When Go

MW01101897

WHEN
GOD
SEEMS
FAR AWAY

JOY JACOBS

CHRISTIAN PUBLICATIONS, INC.
CAMP HILL, PENNSYLVANIA

To Ruth Dourte,
my counselor and my friend,
and to Mom and Pap Clever,
the best grandparents my little boy could possibly have.

My sincere thanks to:
- My husband, Bob, and our three sons, who lived with me through it all.
- Terry Middlekauff, who typed the entire manuscript as an act of love.
- Sally Walker, who proofread and encouraged.
- Dr. Arnie Fleagle, our pastor, who was never too busy to look up a Hebrew Word.
- Jinny Muir, who counseled me to write this book in God's timing, not mine.
- Dawn Sundquist, my editor, whose careful and courteous criticims enabled the truth to be more clearly stated.

The stories and illustrations in this book are based on actual experiences. However, the names of persons involved have been changed to protect confidentiality.

⚏ CHRISTIAN PUBLICATIONS, INC.

3825 Hartzdale Drive, Camp Hill, PA 17011
www.christianpublications.com

Faithful, biblical publishing since 1883

When God Seems Far Away
ISBN: 0-87509-403-1
LOC Control Number: 88-71947
© 1988 by Joy Jacobs
All rights reserved
Printed in the United States of America

04   05   06   07   08   9   8   7   6   5

Weeping may endure for a night,
but joy comes in the morning.

PSALM 30:5

CONTENTS

FOREWORD

It is a rare writer indeed who can take personalities in Scripture and describe them in such a way that they seem to be neighbors, friends, or even members of our own family.

Joy has succeeded in such a far-reaching challenge. She has exposed the hurts of our brothers and sisters in biblical times and shown the paths they took to survival. Successfully tying in the hurts of her own past, she gives us fresh incentives for survival and practical counsel to implement into the working-out of our faith. She helps us maintain a tender, teachable spirit—so crucial if we are to be sensitive to the still, small voice of our Father.

Her style is direct and incisive. May it enlighten us in the midst of the fog of subjectivity and broaden our view of life beyond the immediate. . . .

Christine Wyrtzen

1

Why Don't I Feel God's Presence?

ELOHIM-JEHOVAH:
The Creator who is
righteousness, holiness,
and love

"God gave me your name, Joy." My mother's smile seemed to fill the small living room of the trailer in which we lived. "The verse came to me so clearly the day you were born."

She leafed through the worn, dog-eared pages to show me the passage. I bent forward anxiously, eager as always to hear the familiar story. Her long, slim fingers pointed out the verse.

As always, one word seemed more prominent than all the rest.

And the ransomed of the Lord shall return, and come to Zion with songs and everlasting joy upon their heads: they shall obtain joy *and gladness, and sorrow and sighing shall flee away. (Isa. 35:10, KJV, emphasis mine)*

My mother sighed heavily and looked out the window into the cornfield next to our trailer. "In spite of all the problems, Joy, God gave me that assurance."

My childish mind wasn't sure what problems she meant,

but I knew there had always been problems in our family. Especially in the past few years, when Daddy was angry so often.

I was never quite sure *why.* Sometimes the anger would come on so suddenly, seemingly without cause, and I would retreat into the back bedroom. Usually I would bury myself in a book, closing the sliding door, my ears, and my mind to what followed. But often I couldn't avoid hearing.

Sometimes, even when I thought everything was going well, I would realize that my father was unusually quiet. Glancing at him, I would see his face contorted into a terrible expression of anger, and at times I could actually hear him gritting his teeth.

Why? What happened? I wondered. I would avoid looking at him or again retreat into my fantasy world.

My mother's words continued. "And so, Joy, you must always live up to the meaning of your name. Remember: True joy doesn't depend on circumstances—where we live or how much money we have—but on the peace that the Lord puts within our hearts, in spite of the problems."

Her gaze went beyond the cornfield to the cloud-scattered horizon.

"Weeping may endure for a night," she murmured, "but joy cometh in the morning."

IS IT MORNING YET?

Because I loved my mother more than anyone else in the world, I wanted to bring her pleasure. I did my best to obey her. I *tried* to live up to the meaning of my name.

For many years of my life I searched for that magical, mystical spiritual experience that would somehow make the joy come.

But it always seemed to elude me.

Oh, yes, there were many times when I did feel joyful. And when I didn't, I learned to cover my negative emotions with a smile, to hide them with a laugh.

People often said, "Your mother certainly picked the right name." To avoid feeling hypocritical, I often replied: "You might not say that if you lived with me!"

I didn't share with them the haunting feeling that nights of weeping were inevitable—and more frequent than morning joy.

I wondered about Mother's quiet assurance. I was full of doubts about God's promises, about His goodness, about the gladness of which she spoke.

My conscious mind was programmed to say good things about God, but my unconscious mind projected other images. I thought of Him as a jealous, overprotective Being who cared little about my feelings, my abilities, my desires.

I believed that He was my Creator. But I didn't recognize that He had also created those feelings, those abilities—even many of those desires.

Looking back, I realize that God seemed very much like my father. And I wanted to get away from my earthly father.

Which is one reason why I had a very limited understanding of the character of my heavenly Father.

WHO ARE YOU, GOD?

Stop and think about *your* name. Do you know its meaning?

In Old Testament times, names were so important that children were sometimes given a temporary name at birth, then renamed later in accordance with their personality or character.

The Old Testament people, the Hebrews, called their God by many different names. Why? Because no one word was adequate to describe His greatness. Unfortunately, the Old Testament as we have it today does not give us the advantage of getting to know God through the original Hebrew names; they are simply translated as God, Lord, or God Almighty.

Missionaries and translators have always had difficulty in finding a suitable word for God. They still experience the frustration Moses felt when he asked: "Who are You, God? What is the meaning of Your name?"

Dr. James Packer points out that "ignorance of God—ignorance both of his ways and of the practice of communion with him—lies at the root of much of the church's weakness today. . . . *Christian minds have been conformed to the modern spirit*: the spirit, that is, that spawns great thought of man and leaves room for only small thoughts of God."[1]

How do we come to understand the character of God?

I believe the most basic beginning is to learn the meanings of His name.

The Hebrew name for the Creator-God was "the Elohim." In the first chapter of Genesis, prior to the creation of Adam and Eve, the word Elohim was mentioned thirty-five times. Elohim is a plural noun, indicating to some scholars the presence of the Trinity during Creation. This name for God carries with it a sense of God's greatness and glory, His creative and governing power, His omnipotence and sovereignty.

In Genesis 2:4, however, where we begin to learn more about Adam and Eve, the name "Jehovah" is used for the first time. Jehovah is a God of moral and spiritual attributes. He is a God of righteousness and holiness.

Jehovah is to have a special relationship with people. He desires to commune with this man and woman He has created, to have fellowship with them, to enjoy them in a different way from the way He enjoys the animals and the rest of creation.

"So God created man in His own image" (Gen. 1:27).

Elohim is great and glorious; Jehovah is righteous and holy. Adam and Eve were created in God's image of greatness and glory *and* of righteousness and holiness.

It was against God's righteousness and holiness that Eve sinned when she listened to the serpent. Consequently, the greatness and glory God had given His creation were lost. A righteous Jehovah whose holiness was violated was forced to condemn unrighteousness—and to punish it.

So Eve had to leave the Garden and enter a wilderness.

But the name Jehovah has another meaning. Jehovah is not only the God of righteousness and holiness but also the God of love.

The name Jehovah is rooted in the Hebrew word *havah,* meaning "to be" or "being" or "I am becoming." As a child I was fascinated by those strange biblical words in capital letters—"I AM THAT I AM"—but I did not understand their meaning.

What a delight to discover that another translation of the name Jehovah is "I am becoming all that you need."

In Jeremiah 31:3 this Jehovah says: "Yea, I have loved thee with an everlasting love: therefore with loving-kindness have I drawn thee" (KJV). Love constrained Elohim to seek Adam and Eve, those He had created—even after they had sinned.

And ages later Jehovah came seeking once again. The Elohim-Jehovah sacrificed part of Himself in a once-for-all Day of Atonement. He shared the grief and suffering of all those He had created. As a result, Jesus Christ, the ultimate Sacrifice-Substitute for sin and sinners, is available to each of us.

But first we must see our need.

That need, however, is often blocked by our image of God. And our image of God is often entangled with our perceptions of our earthly parents.

MY FATHER-IMAGE

As a teenager, I rejected my father. Because of his work as a salesman, we moved often, so often that I took a correspondence course in lieu of attending public school. Our family never owned a home; we lived in inadequate trailers and cheap, unattractive apartments. My brother and I were not able to attend a Sunday school class regularly or become involved in any youth activities, not even Christian ones. I was not allowed to stay overnight at the homes of friends or relatives. We didn't even have a TV!

Because of my father, I was different from everyone else. My mother was very understanding of the desires of a normal adolescent, but would not countermand Dad's authority. He frequently threatened suicide if his disapproval or anger did not produce the desired results.

I became increasingly resentful toward Dad. I repressed my rebellion, however, because my mother always seemed to bear the brunt of his anger.

During those difficult teenage years, I did not understand my father at all. I can remember lying in bed at night and wishing he would not come home, thinking how much happier life would be without him. Then I would experience guilt and fear, wondering how God would judge me for my sinful thoughts.

Looking back from an adult perspective, I can understand my father much better. As the oldest of six children—four sisters and then a little brother—Dad worked very hard for very little reward with his father on a Pennsylvania Dutch farm. Dad and my grandfather also took a coal train to the mines early each morning.

One morning a dynamite explosion took my grandfather's life. It also left permanent physical and emotional scars on my father. At the age of nineteen, Dad was temporarily blinded; his head, I was told, swelled to the size of a bushel basket. The bluish coal marks left their imprint on his face for life—and fear and frustration left their imprint on his emotions.

Since the correspondence course I took was accelerated, I graduated from high school at the age of sixteen, having attended nine different schools. Dad was not ready for me to make college plans, but I was ready. Because of the intervention of my high school principal and English teacher, I was able to make arrangements to attend Messiah College, helped by numerous scholarships, loans, and grants.

As a very immature seventeen-year-old freshman, I attended a voice recital with a date and listened to a basketball player named Bob Jacobs render his recital piece: "Open the Gates of the Temple." Although my original impression, confirmed by the dorm mother, was that the guy was "way too old for me," the song must have opened the gates of my heart! I broke up with my date the next day and started "Bob-watching."

Bob had headed for college after meeting the Lord in Panama City, Florida, while in the Air Force. He was more than seven years my senior. His maturity (at least in some areas!), his singing ability, and his outgoing personality greatly impressed me. We soon began dating during the week; I was proud of the fact that he was already singing with his brothers every weekend. I did my studying while he was out singing and reasoned that, unlike so many guys my own age, Bob knew what he wanted in life!

We saw each other every day; soon we were convinced that one of the things we both wanted was marriage. Without my father's blessing, we were married secretly before my graduation. I was still afraid of what Dad might do if he knew I had deliberately disobeyed him.

Bob and I lived separately and kept our secret for some time. Gradually the news leaked out and our friends and Bob's family participated in a reception for us. What a way to begin a marriage!

MY THREE R'S

All of us have three "r's" to deal with. I'm not referring to readin', 'ritin', and 'rithmetic. Those three r's were no problem for me. But I did have a great deal of trouble with another set: roots, relationships, and responsibilities.

As a teenager, I had rejected my roots—a father who

seemed insensitive to my needs and goals. I realize now that my relationship with him had a lasting influence on my relationship with my heavenly Father. Old Testament verses that spoke of a "jealous God" haunted my feeble attempts to communicate with that other Father. This unknown Being, like my own father, seemed domineering, angry, and distant, even when I tried so hard to be good.

My father had been overprotective and jealous; at the age of nineteen, I married a man who was just the opposite. The ministry in which my husband was involved took him away from me often, sometimes for long stretches of time—and he seemed to enjoy every minute of it!

And I, who had longed for freedom in my teenage years, found that my new freedom left me feeling—again— terribly insecure.

But it was time for new responsibilities.

For the first three years of our marriage I was able to travel with my husband on occasion, but then life changed drastically with two "blessed events." I gave birth to two active, healthy little boys within fourteen months of each other.

ENCOUNTERS WITH THE SERPENT

Gradually, my insecurity bred anxiety and resentment. Like Ancestress Eve, I listened to the serpent.

And the wily serpent whispered: "Can it really be that God has called only your husband into ministry? Are you not also intelligent? Do you not have a college degree? Look how mundane *your* work is, compared to his. While he travels and sings and meets new people, does God expect you to be content with bottles and diapers—and bills?"

Eve's daughter protested: "But I *know* that God has called him."

"Perhaps-s-s," hissed the serpent. "But s-s-surely He has called you too. Think of all the honors you were given in high school and college. Think on these things."

"Did God really say that
You must not eat from any tree?
Perhaps you heard Him wrong,
Misunderstood His meaning."
The serpent's words penetrated,
confused my mind, beguiled my thoughts.
What had God really said?
Surely His rules were flexible.
This situation's different.
God will understand.[2]

And like Eve, Eve's daughter began to ponder these things. And she ate of the tree of resentment, and the root of bitterness, whose seed had been sown in earlier years, took hold and began to grow. And her garden became a wilderness dominated by thorns and thistles.

SCREAMS IN THE DESERT

It was easy to start feeling sorry for myself again, to slip back into familiar patterns of negative reactions. My excitement at becoming a mother had turned to anxiety over financial problems and the growing feeling that no one was too concerned about *my* personal needs. I had not been able to communicate with my father and gradually, over a period of years, I gave up on trying to communicate my true feelings to my husband. Resentment led me to withdraw from taking an active part in my husband's ministry; financial pressure gave me a valid reason for finding work where my value would be appreciated.

A wilderness is a kind of desert, an uncultivated region through which we wander hopelessly, aimlessly, like the children of Israel, in forty-year follies. The thorns and thistles I discovered in my wilderness became more and more entangled—and entangling. I screamed for help, but those around me didn't seem to hear. My patterns of thinking developed into deep ruts. Gradually my negative attitudes led to sinful actions.

But the fruit of the tree of resentment had turned rotten between my teeth. I longed to disentangle myself from the thorns and thistles. I had wandered in the wilderness long enough—far too long. I desired communion with my Creator.

CONFRONTATIONS—VERTICAL AND HORIZONTAL

I had not felt sure of God's love, however, when I was "good." Could this perfect God love me now, when I was "bad"?

The serpent was back. "S-s-silly girl!" he hissed. "Of course not! God's perfect—you said it yourself! So you might as well keep on sinning. It's too late now!"

Was it too late? Could the ruts be reversed, the barriers broken? I longed to communicate in a real way with those around me—and with the Father God who had created me. I yearned to know Him as He really was.

But He was perfect . . . and I was far from being perfect.

Yet it was the very awareness of sin in my life that inspired the yearning to know God. All the "trying to be good" had gotten me nowhere; it simply fortified the walls between me and the people who didn't seem to be trying as hard as I was.

In a seminar I attended it was pointed out that, although there were people in my life who had wronged me, my resentment toward them was just as wrong. My resentment, reinforced by my anxiety that my needs would not be supplied, was sin. Sinful actions had merely followed sinful attitudes in a logical assembly line.

My thinking and attitudes had to be dealt with! I confessed them to God and asked His forgiveness.

I was encouraged to make a list of the people toward whom I had wrong attitudes. My total came to seventeen. The next step involved confession (to people) and retribution, where necessary. We were directed to deal with the longest-standing problem first.

I knew I needed to talk to my father.

In September of 1975 I did something I had never imagined I would do. I asked my father's forgiveness for my bitterness toward him. Three months later he injured himself in a fall and went into a coma from which he never awoke. I had listened to my heavenly Father's direction just in time.

My list involved other family members, including my husband. We discussed the surface problems, but I knew there were deeper layers that had not been touched. But how? And when? Time was needed to penetrate the real issues, and we were too pressured to carve that kind of time out of our busy schedules.

On the surface, things looked pretty good. I had a hard-working, faithful, beginning-to-be-successful husband and two bright, healthy sons. I was teaching part-time and also working as an editor, bringing proofreading home at night. I plastered on my expected smile and kept moving.

But inside I was still very insecure. I was still hurting deeply. There were days when I wondered if I loved my husband. And I was still resentful toward the ministry that constantly took him away from me and our sons.

The serpent was whispering again: "S-s-silly girl! You and your husband are two totally different personalities! You're different in every possible way! Don't try to tell him how you're *really* feeling. He'd never understand—and God doesn't understand either!"

Yet I longed to know God . . . as He really is.

Like Eve, I had entered a wilderness. But in my wilderness I had seen my need of a righteous and holy God who would love me still. And that great Jehovah came seeking me.

God has unique ways of dealing with each of us. This great and glorious Elohim-Jehovah, in addition to His creative imagination (just look at the variety He has created!), has a wonderful sense of humor.

Remember Miriam, the "I-am-Miriam-I-am-right" sister

of Moses and Aaron, who found her critical spirit and bitterness chastened by the dreaded disease of leprosy? Well, Miriam and I will reminisce together in heaven! At the age of twenty-nine I was struck down with the undignified curse of chicken pox.

Miriam was banished from the camp until her leprosy was cured. I felt just as much of an outcast. Scabs literally covered my face and scalp. I couldn't wash my hair for two weeks. For three weeks I was deathly sick, so helplessly sick I could hardly get from my bedroom to the bathroom, much less take care of my not-as-sick children.

I looked in the mirror and thought: "Ugh! Ugly!"

And I began to see that there was still ugliness inside.

God's sense of humor? His perfect timing? Only one reason has ever kept my itinerant husband at home in bed for more than a day or two, and that is a recurring back problem. Sure enough, those back muscles collapsed during the second week I was confined to bed.

Bob was in so much pain that he couldn't move. I was pathetically weak and ugly. Bob's mother, who lived next door, brought in meals and took care of our poxy kids.

We couldn't walk away from each other, as we had been doing for so long. We were forced to talk to each other— for a whole week!

We talked. We cried. We began to penetrate more than surface issues. We recognized wrongs. We confessed to each other. We confessed to the Lord.

We forgave. He forgave.

The God of righteousness and holiness was at work. The God of love was healing our marriage.

To be completely honest, I must add that it was the *start* of a healing. We were still two stubborn Pennsylvania Dutchmen, accustomed to heading in two different directions. We did not take orders from the Lord very well. Unlike the chicken pox, the chastening did not end in two or three weeks.

Someone has said that we are not so much punished *for*

our sin as *by* our sin. We found that to be true.

But the healing had begun! I had recognized my sin. I had acknowledged my need. I was beginning to realize that God—and my husband—had seen me at my worst, physically and spiritually, and both of them loved me in spite of it!

I was beginning to understand true security in the assurance of my Creator's love.

The great and glorious Elohim-Jehovah, the sovereign God of creation, of righteousness, of holiness and love, redemptively works through history—His story—and our personal histories as well to accomplish His purposes!

WHAT IS THE MEANING OF HIS NAME?

1. In the first usage of Elohim in Genesis 1:1, what was said about the nature of God?

2. The word Elohim is plural, as becomes obvious in Genesis 1:26; 3:22; 11:7. Some scholars interpret this plurality as an early introduction to the concept of the Trinity: God the Father, God the Son, and God the Holy Spirit. If this were the case, what can we infer about God's relationship with Jesus? The Holy Spirit? Why is it wrong to emphasize the importance of one member of the Trinity to the exclusion of the other two?

3. After Elohim spoke to Noah in Genesis 6, how do you suppose Noah's wife felt about her husband's new carpentry project? What might the neighbors have said to add to her feelings of insecurity?

4. Sarah, the wife of Abraham, was ninety years old when Elohim renewed His promise of a son in Genesis 17:7. Imagine her reaction to God's mention of their heirs. How would you feel?

5. How is Elohim described in the following passages: Deuteronomy 10:17-18; Psalm 7:9; Psalm 57:2; Psalm 91:2; Isaiah 45:5-12? How do these attributes of God affect

you personally as His child? How do they affect the feelings of insecurity you might have?

6. The name Jehovah (from the Hebrew word *havah*—"to be" or "being") describes the One who always exists, the eternal and unchangeable One. (See Ps. 102:25-27.) Read or sing the words of the song "Great Is Thy Faithfulness" daily this week.

7. When God created people "in His own image" (Gen. 1:27), He gave them the capacity to enjoy fellowship with Him. Sin destroyed this fellowship, but faith in Jesus Christ restores it and allows us to put on the "new nature," again created in God's image. What attributes of this new nature are named in Ephesians 4:24?

8. The name Jehovah was so honored by the Jewish people that they never read it in the synagogue or even uttered it. As a result, the original pronunciation has been lost. What penalty was imposed on those who used irreverently the holy name of Jehovah? (See Lev. 24:16.)

9. List the attributes of Jehovah given in Exodus 34:5-7, both positive and negative. Why does it say that He forgives iniquity, but avenges the sins of fathers upon their children "unto the third and to the fourth generation"? (Think about the lingering effects of "sins of the fathers" and the statement: "We are not so much punished *for* our sins as *by* our sins.")

10. What sins need to be confessed and cleared from your life so that they will not affect *your* family members—or your relationship with a holy Jehovah?

11. Read Psalm 103 and memorize verse 12: "As far as the east is from the west, so far has He removed our transgressions from us."

2

*Why Is Life So
Empty of Meaning?*

EL SHADDAI:
The all-sufficient One
JEHOVAH-JIREH:
The provider

When the serpent tempted Eve to question God's laws for
life, Eve listened. Genesis 3 tells of the result: great hurt to
herself, as well as to all the future daughters of Eve. In
losing her fellowship with her Creator, Eve also lost the
sense of security He had planned for her. No longer did she
feel accepted, known, loved. Immediately she began to try
to cover her nakedness, emotional as well as physical.

Daughters of Eve have been following her example ever
since.

One of them was Sarai, whose name was later changed
to Sarah. Her first name is thought to have meant "the
contentious one." Her new name meant "princess."
Between those two names was an agonizing struggle.

SARAI'S INSECURITY

I think it's safe to surmise that Abram, whose name was
also changed, touched a raw nerve early in his marriage
when he announced God's plan to his lovely wife: They

were going to leave the fond and familiar to follow some
unsavory-smelling camels through a dry, deserted land
to—where? Abram didn't know! Sarai must have felt like
screaming!

"Believe, my love, you must believe!" he says.
Would he believe if this strange God
Had spoken to me instead?
It's all so hard to understand.
How can I know that it was God who spoke
And not some strange nightmare?[1]

What was Sarai leaving behind? She and Abram, as half-
brother and sister, grew up together in the metropolis of Ur,
and Sarai may have lived in a two-story, balconied house,
with polished stone floors covered by oriental rugs.

When Sarai left Ur, she left her life-long home. With it
she left her sense of identity. At their first stopping-off
point, Haran (located midway across the Fertile Crescent),
she left behind her father, who had begun to accompany
them on their strange journey. Her feelings of insecurity
probably increased with the loss of his advice and
leadership.

And as she watched the children in the camel caravan—
the servants' children—Sarai was constantly reminded of
one fact. Her friends back in Ur were enjoying their
grandchildren, and she had not given Abram a son!

In days when fertility was considered a sign of the deity's
favor, barrenness was the supreme humiliation. A woman
without a child had no real purpose in life, no hope for the
future.

Without a home and a child, Sarai had no significance.

SECURITY AND SIGNIFICANCE
Unlike Sarai, contemporary women live in a day of
multiple options. Equal education and careers are open to

us. Yet with the smorgasbord of choices before us, we still struggle with a sense of worthlessness.

Dr. Lawrence Crabb, a Christian psychologist, expresses it well:

People have one basic personal need which requires two kinds of input for its satisfaction. The most basic need is a sense of personal worth, an acceptance of oneself as a whole, real person. The two required inputs are significance *(purpose, importance, adequacy for a job, meaningfulness, impact) and* security *(love—unconditional and consistently expressed; permanent acceptance).* [2]

At least, you may say, Sarai had the security of her husband's love—and it is a well-known fact that she was beautiful.

Yes, but . . . ! Sarai's beauty was so obvious that her loving husband twice passed her off as his sister—a half-truth, since they did have the same father—to save his own neck. Abram was afraid the Pharaoh—and later, a local chieftain—would kill him and then take her as his wife; he fell prey to his own cowardice instead, and Sarai spent some anxiety-filled nights in two men's harems. Is that security?

God stepped in and delivered Sarai before her purity was compromised. But still there was no child. When they left Haran, Sarai was sixty-five and her husband, seventy-five. For years God promised and continued to remind Abram that his descendants would be as countless as the stars, but the fulfillment of His promises seemed as far away and nebulous as the heavenly bodies themselves.

"Wait," Abram says, "believe and wait!"
I've waited ten long years
And many more before God's promise.
It seems my husband's God could use some help.
The marriage contract I signed long ago

Contained a promise I'd provide my husband with a son.
It's custom for a barren wife
To give life through a slave.
This aged body will never live again. [3]

And so, in Genesis 16, Hagar enters. An Egyptian slave-girl, she was perhaps torn from her home and the worship of Isis (the goddess of the earth and therefore fertility), joined to the strange caravan, and forced to become a surrogate mother. Sarai, probably feeling she was fulfilling her marital duty to Abram, gave Hagar to her husband in a desperate attempt to have a son by the slave girl. Hagar's son would be considered legally Sarai's.

When Hagar discovered that she was with child, however, her arrogance only increased Sarai's feelings of worthlessness. Sarai, defensive and contentious, dealt severely with Hagar. Finally Hagar fled into the desert-wilderness.

Two insecure, insignificant women . . .

SEARCHING FOR SIGNIFICANCE

In the first chapter I shared some of my struggles with insecurity; I also struggled with overwhelming feelings of insignificance—especially when people praised my husband's ministry.

In college I had prepared to be an English teacher. Instead, after graduation, I did secretarial work for my husband, mothered our children, and worked at various part-time jobs to bring in extra income.

I knew that my support was important to Bob, but helping him just didn't seem to make my life meaningful enough to satisfy me completely. The part-time jobs I held only added busyness and frustration to my life.

I needed to learn to exercise the gifts God had given me, but at that point I didn't know what they were.

And, more important, I needed to get to know the Giver better.

ENCOUNTERS WITH GOD

Karen Mains asks a searching question:

*How do we—mundane, ordinary, everyday beings—come to
know God in such a way that our lives can accomplish deeds of
spiritual significance? How can we know Him so well that we
can be assured He will answer our prayer for fire on the altar as
He did for the audacious Elijah? How can we come to know God
closely enough to interpret the dream of prophecy like the bold
Joseph? How does this intimate knowledge come—the kind that
stimulates these exploits?*

*I am convinced that this kind of knowing comes through a
familiarity with the Godhead bred through the hundreds of
common incidents in our lives. It is these encounters which God
chooses to infuse with His presence* and which we then must
take the time to recognize as vehicles of himself. *The bush
flamed, if you will remember. It was alive with the Presence, but
Moses had to turn aside to see. So must we.*[4]

I will always be thankful that Bob and I recognized the
illnesses described in the first chapter as encounters with
God. We are also thankful that God gave us wisdom to
discern His direction. During the third week of the "chicken
pox chastening," we decided that I should quit both of my
part-time jobs and use my writing skills in support of the
music ministry that my husband shared with his brothers.
God blessed that decision in many ways.

Another encounter with God surprised us a year later. I
began an unexpected, unplanned pregnancy—despite an
IUD. My gynecologist suggested I have a D & C rather than
a pregnancy test, stating "it was too early to matter." The
IUD could become entangled in the placenta, he explained,
but the IUD could not be removed without possible injury
to the placenta. The easiest way out was to scrape the
uterus, thus removing the IUD—but also the fetus. In
effect, he was suggesting a therapeutic abortion, although
the word abortion was not used.

Unlike Sarai, I had not been depending on the birth of a

child for significance! Our small, two-bedroom home was already full to overflowing. I had been looking forward to this year of freedom; for the first time our sons Robbie and Ricky would attend school all day. Financially, we certainly were not prepared for another child, and I had given all my baby things away.

One more concern threw a shadow across this pregnancy. My husband's youngest brother, who lived next door to us with my widowed mother-in-law, was severely retarded. His presence regularly reminded me of my fear that our child would be abnormal in some way. Could the doctor be right in suggesting that it was, indeed, "too early to matter"? Would we eliminate a lot of future problems by simply following his suggestion and terminating the pregnancy?

God's Word becomes very precious in times of crisis. Psalm 139 burned itself into my consciousness:

For thou hast possessed my [inward parts]; thou hast covered me in my mother's womb.

I will praise thee; for I am fearfully and wonderfully made. . . .

My substance was not hid from thee, when I was made in secret, and [intricately] wrought in the lowest parts of the earth.

Thine eyes did see my substance, yet being [unformed]; and in thy book all my members were written, which in continuance were fashioned, when as yet there was none of them. (Ps. 139:13-16, KJV)

God's opinion was obvious; there was really no decision to be made! I was ordered to stay off my feet as much as possible, especially during the first trimester, and we began turning a laundry room into a nursery.

Little David was born a month late by the doctor's estimate, but in God's perfect timing. He was perfectly normal. (The IUD was birthed right after David.)

That year—1976—was also the year my father died, and

we felt the Lord leading us to move my mother into one of the two trailers on our property that we had been using as rentals. Again our budget would be unbalanced, but I was thrilled to have my mother so close, and the boys were excited about having two grandmas within walking distance. Yes, God's leading was again very obvious!

Encounters with God, however, are not always easily understood. I was probably too busy to be perceptive of my mother's concerns about everything that was happening. And so she delayed in telling me that she had found a lump in her breast. She delayed so long in telling me *and* her new doctor that the breast was almost ready to ulcerate when he finally became aware of the problem.

After that fateful doctor's appointment, she told me she was scheduled for surgery the next day. I had been sitting in the car, waiting for my mother, nursing my baby. Her words shattered my world.

"He called the hospital to schedule surgery as soon as possible, Joy, but it's possible that the cancer has already spread into the lymphatic system."

"Mother, *why*—why didn't you tell me earlier?"

"Joy, twenty years ago I found a lump in my breast. I was prayed for and it disappeared. I felt as though telling the doctor was denying God's healing power. And you were so busy, Joy . . . I hated to bother you."

In the next few weeks I realized, perhaps for the first time, how much I had depended on my mother as a role model for so many years. Often I had gone into her bedroom to find her kneeling beside the bed, praying. Or I had come home from school to find her sitting at the table, studying her worn, well-marked Bible, with commentaries spread around her.

My mother never met a stranger. She was loved by everyone who knew her, especially children. Although her life was a series of uprootings and conflicts, she possessed a settled peace of mind. I know intuitively that her secret was her deep faith in Jesus Christ as her Savior and Lord; she had committed her life to Him at the age of twenty-one and, despite the erratic life-style she married into, she never wavered in her commitment to my father or to her heavenly Father.

Then *why* had He rewarded her in this way? After nursing my father for the last ten years of his life, she deserved some rest, a time of carefree happiness. Why, God, why?

I well remember the night I sat in darkness in my front yard, looking up at the stars—the very same stars that God had used to illustrate His promises to Abram and Sarai.

But I felt like Sarai. To me, that angry night, God's promises seemed a mockery of everything my mother had lived and taught.

Mother loved to paraphrase Scripture, and the ninety-first Psalm was one of her favorites:

[She]* that dwelleth in the secret place of the Most High shall abide under the shadow of the Almighty. I will say of the Lord, He is my refuge and my fortress, my God; in Him will I trust. Surely He will deliver thee from the . . . deadly pestilence. (Ps. 91:1-3, KJV)

Where were God's promises? I asked angrily. *Where was His deliverance? What more "deadly pestilence" could there be than cancer?*

I felt like throwing stones at the silent sky.

People might have reproved and admonished me had I told them my feelings. But God didn't. Instead, in His time, He touched and healed my angry, hurting spirit.

Time after time I took my mother for tests, treatments, checkups, bone scans, doctors' visits, more tests, more treatments. I cannot remember her complaining once. Instead, she took advantage of every possible

---

*"She" is substituted for "He."

opportunity—as she always had—to witness of her faith in Jesus Christ.

She had always been outspoken about her faith. So much so, in fact, that her ready testimony had embarrassed me as a teenager. Now, however, I began to realize that her faith was based not on circumstances or environments, but on the only never-changing factor in her life: "Jesus Christ—the same today, yesterday, and forever."

I also began to realize the limitations of my own faith: "For My thoughts are not your thoughts, neither are your ways My ways, says the Lord" (Isa. 55:8).

God spared my mother for another eight years of relatively good health, but her illness led, indirectly, to another encounter with God. Someone has said that such events are not coincidences, but God-incidences.

While waiting for her to undergo tests at the hospital one day, I visited the local Christian bookstore and talked with the manager, Larry Hair. When I got up the nerve to ask him if he would be interested in carrying a booklet containing a series of articles I had written for my husband's ministry newsletter—*if* I could get it printed on my own—he suggested I contact Christian Publications, the publishing arm of our denomination.

"Forget it, Larry!" I remember saying. "I don't know anybody there. And besides, they only publish preachers and missionaries—not a nobody like me."

"Try it," Larry urged.

I didn't have enough courage to call the editor, as Larry had suggested, so I wrote him a letter, enclosing some articles I had written. Dr. Keith Bailey, then editor of Christian Publications, called me within the week for an interview. He was looking for a writer for a women's devotional book. Would I be interested?

Would I? I jumped at the chance, suggesting the topic of Bible women, on whom I had already done some research. Dr. Bailey requested twelve sample chapters for inspection

by the review committee. Within several more months I
was under contract to write a 365-page devotional!

Now I know that it was not a committee's decision, but a
commission from God, an assignment that would change
the direction of my life. It was not until much later that I
realized what had happened to me in the process of
writing. For almost two years I turned off the TV and
devoted my spare moments to studying, researching,
delving into God's Word. The Word began to saturate my
mind. Although it would take even more time to be
absorbed into my life-style, it began to cleanse my thought
patterns, the first step in a permanent change of my
attitudes and actions.

The Word who had become flesh and dwelt among us
was now dwelling within me. My encounters with God
were being reinforced by a growing knowledge of God.

But there was still so much more to learn about Him.

JEHOVAH-JIREH: PRE-VISION AND PROVISION
We've left Hagar in the desert-wilderness. Picture this all-
alone, terrified slave-girl sitting by a spring of water in the
wilderness, perhaps trying to find a way to take the
precious water with her as she contemplates the all-
consuming thirst ahead during her long trip across desert
sand. Back to her home, Egypt. Back to the worship of the
images of Isis, who held the *ankh,* the symbol of life, in her
hand.

At least Egyptian worship, unlike Abram's invisible God,
provided something to see and to touch, Hagar might have
thought to herself.

But wait! Who was this approaching, even speaking to
her?

*But the Angel of the Lord found her by a spring of water in the
wilderness. . . .*
And He said, Hagar, Sarai's maid, where did you come from,

and where are you intending to go? And she said, I am running away from my mistress Sarai.

The Angel of the Lord said to her, Go back to your mistress and (humbly) submit to her control. (Gen. 16:7-9)

Who was this "Angel of the Lord" who spoke so authoritatively? When an angel appeared on another occasion in the Old Testament, he was called a "redeeming Angel" or "the Angel the Redeemer." Could it have been Christ Himself who appeared to Hagar?

The Angel had more to say:

I will multiply your descendants exceedingly so that they shall not be numbered for multitude. . . . See now, you are with child, and shall bear a son, and shall call his name Ishmael [that is, God hears]; because the Lord has heard and paid attention to your affliction.

Therefore the well was called Beer-lahai-roi (that is, A well of the Living One Who sees me). (Gen. 16:10-11, 14)

Hagar's words are significant:

"Have I [not] even here [in the wilderness] looked after Him Who sees me [and lived]? Or have I here also seen [the future purposes or designs] of Him Who sees me?" (Gen. 16:13)

God saw Hagar's affliction. He heard her silent screams. And the God who heard and saw also provided.

Because Jehovah-jireh is the God of pre-vision, He is also the God of provision. What He promises, He provides.

In His time. In His own way.

SARAI'S NAME CHANGE

What about Sarai? What hope was there for an eighty-nine-year-old barren woman? No human hope, but still another promise from God, through her aged husband:

When Abram was ninety-nine years old, the Lord appeared to
him and said, "I am God Almighty; walk before me and be
blameless. . . . As for Sarai your wife, you are no longer to call
her Sarai; her name will be Sarah. I will bless her and will
surely give you a son by her. I will bless her so that she will be
the mother of nations; kings of peoples will come from her. . . .
My covenant I will establish with Isaac, whom Sarah will bear to
you by this time next year." (Gen. 17:1, 15-16, 21, NIV)

The meaning of *Sarah* is princess. Sarah had exchanged
luxurious surroundings for a goatskin tent, but God was
not referring to the earthly trappings of royalty.

The Bible does not tell us Sarah's reaction to her
husband's newest revelation. God repeated the prophecy to
Abraham in Genesis 18, possibly because Sarah needed to
hear the promise from the lips of the Lord Himself.

If you were eighty-nine, wouldn't you?

THE FULLNESS OF EL SHADDAI

Most versions of Genesis 17:1 identify God as "the
Almighty God," who asks us to walk perfectly before Him.
But how can I, imperfect as I am, live perfectly before an
Almighty God? The command only increases my feelings of
inadequacy.

Another translation of that verse, however, identifies
God as El Shaddai.

A book entitled *Names of God* lent new meaning to the
name. Although I was familiar with the song "El Shaddai,"
I had not understood the background of this beautiful
Hebrew word.

The word *El* itself is translated "God" some two hundred
fifty times in the Old Testament, especially in circumstances
that indicate God's great power, might, strength, and
prominence. He is "the El of Israel who gives strength and
fullness of might to His people" (Ps. 68:35).

Shaddai *itself occurs forty-eight times in the Old Testament and
is translated "almighty." The other word so like it, and from
which we believe it to be derived, occurs twenty-four times and is
translated "breast." As connected with the word* breast, *the title*
Shaddai *signifies one who nourishes, supplies, satisfies.
Connected with the word for God,* El, *it then becomes the "One
mighty to nourish, satisfy, supply." Naturally with God the idea
would be intensified, and it comes to mean the One who "sheds
forth" and "pours" out sustenance and blessing. In this sense,
then, God is the all-sufficient, the all-bountiful. . . . It is God as
El who helps, but it is God as Shaddai who abundantly blesses
with all manner of blessings, and blessings of the breast.* [5]

Unfortunately, today's society has taken the maternal
beauty that God created in the image of the breast and
turned it into a source of erotic stimulation only. Those of
us who have had the blessing of nursing our children,
however, find this meaning of Shaddai very enlightening.

Combine it with the masculine imagery of power and
strength denoted by *El,* and we see the God who is truly
the all-sufficient One.

See how beautifully El Shaddai is pictured in Isaiah
66:12-14:

*For thus says the Lord, Behold, I will extend peace to her like a
river, and the glory of the nations like an overflowing stream;
then you shall be nursed, you shall be carried on her hip, and be
trotted on her [God's maternal] knees.*

*As one whom his mother comforts, so will I comfort you; you
shall be comforted in Jerusalem.*

*When you see this your heart shall rejoice, your bones shall
flourish like green and tender grass, and the (powerful) hand of
the Lord shall be revealed and known to be with His servants,
and His indignation to be against His enemies.*

Reading this passage gives us El Shaddai's perspective on
our relationship with Him. He does not command us to be

perfect. He knows and understands our frailties, our inadequacies, having been tempted as we are.

My mother's physical weakness was now obvious; even more obvious to me was my own spiritual weakness. And so Paul's enigmatic statement in 2 Corinthians 12 took on new meaning: "When I am weak, then I am strong—the less I have the more I depend on him" (2 Cor. 12:12b, TLB).

In our brokenness, we find in Him our wholeness, our completeness.

I am the Almighty God; walk and live habitually before me, and be perfect—blameless, whole-hearted, complete.
And I will make My covenant (solemn pledge) between Me and you. . . . (Gen. 17:1-2)

As we walk and live continually in His presence, baring our souls to Him—even our anger at times—He shows us the fullness of El Shaddai.

Sometimes we see El's strength and power. Sometimes we hear the still small voice of the Shaddai, coming to us gently in the night like a nursing mother.

Is anything too hard or too wonderful for the Lord? At the appointed time, when the season [for her delivery] comes around, I will return to you and Sarah shall have borne a son. (Gen. 18:14)

"At the appointed time" . . . in His time.

At the appointed time, Isaac was born. Sarah's life now had significance. At least temporarily.

CONTENTION TO CONTENTMENT

Sarah's name had been changed from "the contentious one" to "princess," but probably she still tended to be contentious. Patterns of thinking are difficult to change.

Hagar had returned after her encounter with God, but

now the child whose birth Sarai had arranged—Ishmael—complicated Sarah's life. By the time Isaac was weaned, Ishmael was a teenager, probably and quite understandably a jealous one. Sarah couldn't handle the interaction between the two boys; Hagar received the brunt of her frustration, and eventually Sarah banished her.

And she wandered on [aimlessly], and lost her way in the wilderness. . . .

When the water in the bottle was all gone, Hagar caused the youth to lie down under one of the shrubs.

Then she went, and sat down opposite him a good way off, about a bow-shot; for she said, Let me not see the death of the lad. And as she sat over opposite him, he lifted up his voice and wept and she raised her voice and wept. (Gen. 21:14b-16)

God heard their cries.

And God heard the voice of the youth, and the Angel of God called to Hagar out of Heaven, and said to her, What troubles you, Hagar? Fear not, for God has heard the voice of the youth where he is.

Arise, raise up the youth and support him . . . for I intend to make him a great nation.

Then God opened her eyes and she saw a well of water; and she went and filled the [empty] bottle with water, and caused the youth to drink.

And God was with the youth; and he developed and dwelt in the wilderness. (Gen. 21:17-20)

Again, God had heard the voice of a seemingly insignificant slave girl. Jehovah-jireh had seen her affliction and had provided. In Hagar's insufficiency, El Shaddai had proved His sufficiency.

This time God did not instruct Hagar to return to her mistress, as He had earlier. But Sarah's peace was short-lived nonetheless. She still had some lessons to learn about her insufficiency. God tested Abraham's obedience by asking him to sacrifice Sarah's son.

When Abraham left for Mount Moriah, the mountain of sacrifice and the center of present-day Jerusalem, at least six tortuous days must have followed for Sarah. If she knew that God had commanded her husband to sacrifice their son, she must have experienced a week of almost unbearable agony. If Abraham did not confide in her, it still would have been a week of terrible uncertainty. Where—and why—had they gone?

"On the third day Abraham looked up and saw the place in the distance" (Gen. 22:4).

Perhaps, in her aloneness, Sarah encountered God in a new way. Perhaps it was the surgery of sacrifice that confirmed the title of princess, that transformed the contentious one into a woman who was finally content. To experience the all-sufficiency of El Shaddai, one must recognize one's own insufficiency.

Christine Wyrtzen sings with understanding of us, the daughters of Sarah:

I've been through a fire
And it's deepened my desire
To know the living God more and more.
It hasn't been much fun,
But the work that it has done
In my life has made it worth the hurt.

You know, sometimes it takes the hard times
To bring us to our knees;
Otherwise, we do as we please and never heed Him.
But He always knows what's best
And it's when we are distressed
That we really come to know God as He is.[6]

And the El Shaddai who gave a son to a couple whose bodies were dead saw and provided. Jehovah-jireh stopped

Abraham's hand from sacrificing his son and provided a ram in the bushes as a substitute sacrifice!

What joy must have filled Sarah's heart as she watched husband and son stride back into camp—the empty camp that quickly became so full of promise and laughter once again.

The "new" Sarah, as described in 1 Peter 3:1-5, led a pure and godly life, with an emphasis on inward rather than outward beauty. Her life had meaning. She had a loving and respectful relationship with her husband and was no longer unnerved by anxieties or hysterical fears, no longer dominated by jealousy and bitterness.

She had become a true princess—a spiritual princess who could survive even in a goatskin tent.

THE HALVES OF WHOLENESS

What is true significance? What gives us lasting security? The luxuries of life? They held no meaning or purpose for Sarah. A loving husband? Sarah's "man of faith" failed her more than once. Status within the neighborhood? Hagar's ability to bear a son gave her more significance than her mistress. Children? Even the laughter surrounding Isaac's birth gave way to old bitterness.

What are the answers to those vital questions for contemporary daughters of Sarah? Is education the answer? A promising career?

Dr. Lawrence Crabb answers with these words:

Significance depends upon understanding who I am in Christ. I will come to feel significant as I have an eternal impact on people around me by ministering to them. . . . As I mature by developing Christlike traits, I will enter more and more fully into the significance of belonging to and serving the Lord.

My need for security demands that I be unconditionally loved, accepted, and cared for, now and forever. God has seen me at my worst and still loved me to the point of giving His life for me. [7]

Like Sarai's, our laughter has had the hollow ring of uncertainty and meaninglessness.

Like lonely Hagar, we have been weeping helplessly in the wilderness.

But Jehovah-jireh has seen and heard—and provided.

And El Shaddai promises: "My name is not 'I was' but 'I AM'! *I am* sufficient to meet your needs."

WHAT IS THE MEANING OF HIS NAME?

1. How old was Abram when God renewed His covenant in Genesis 17:1-16? What was Abram's physical position while God was speaking? (See Gen. 17:3.)

2. What word pictures did God use to describe Abram's descendants? (See Gen. 12:12; 13:16; 15:5.)

3. In Genesis 16, how did Sarai and Abram try to make God's promise come true? What were the results?

4. How should Abraham and Sarah's experience with Hagar affect our evaluation of surrogate motherhood? What immediate and long-lasting effects did Ishmael's birth cause?

5. What is the meaning of the Hebrew word *el*? What is the inferred meaning of the word *shad*? How does your picture of God reconcile these two very different concepts?

6. "Elohim is the God who creates nature so that it is and supports it so that it continues; El Shaddai is the God who compels nature to do what is contrary to itself."[8] How is this truth illustrated in the saga of Sarah?

7. Abraham and Sarah both laughed at the thought of having a child in their old age. What did God say about their heart attitudes? (See Rom. 4:19-21; Heb. 11:11.)

8. At two different times God spoke directly to Hagar, assuring her that He was aware of her needs. Not many other women have experienced this honor. Does this have any personal significance to you?

9. With God, to see is also to foresee, so that pre-vision is provision. How did Hagar first realize that God saw her? (See Gen. 16:8.)

10. Why do you suppose God asked Hagar where she had come from and where she was going? What did He tell her to do?

11. In Genesis 21 Hagar leaves Abraham's camp for the second time, and again God shows her that He is aware of her needs. Why do you suppose God may have spoken to her a second time? (Ishmael is described as a "youth" in some versions.)

12. How has this chapter affected your concept of what it means to be significant? What gives meaning to *your* life? Perhaps it would help you to answer these question by completing this sentence: "I feel as though my life is meaningful when I am _____."

13. Significance will arise out of understanding who we are in Christ: servants of God who can have an eternal impact on people around us. Ask God what special gifts He has given you to use in ministry, then listen quietly for His answer. Be aware of gifts like helps, hospitality, and honesty.

3

How Much Does God Expect of Me?

JEHOVAH-RAAH: The Good Shepherd

My husband helped me into the doctor's office, uncertain how to handle this dizzy brunette who was usually so independent. I had been experiencing periods of light-headedness for several years, but this last attack had frightened me. While running up and down the steps on a hot summer day, between loads of wash and the normal interruptions of three active home-for-the-summer boys, I felt as if I were blacking out completely. My heartbeat seemed to be racing out of control.

After he examined me, my concerned doctor apologized. "Having had your mother as a patient and knowing your father had problems with high blood pressure, I should have realized that you would have hereditary tendencies in that direction. Your blood pressure is much higher than it should be at your age; we need to work at getting it down!"

I was devastated. Having high blood pressure seemed like a fate worse than death. Because it could result in a stroke or other damage to my body? No, I hadn't comprehended all that.

I was most concerned about its emotional implications.

Childhood memories flooded my mind: "Joy, don't upset your dad—his blood pressure is already up!" The words echoed clearly, like remnants of yesterday instead of yester-decade.

Is that what my family members would say about me? "Mom's upset again. Guess her blood pressure's up."

Would my family understand? Would it become obvious to everyone that I wasn't coping well? Would people start walking on eggs around me?

My doctor was asking me a question: "What's the stress level in your life?"

I stared at him blankly. "Stress level? I don't know. Right now I don't know about anything."

His tone was gentle but firm. "Think about it, Joy. Maybe you need to get rid of some of the stress in your life."

That's easy for you to say, I was thinking. *Where do I begin? Do I get rid of my husband—or my kids? All three sons or one at a time?*

Aloud I said, "Our summer camp is in full swing and I have responsibilities there. . . ."

I didn't mention that I had just accepted a full-time teaching position that would begin in another two months.

My doctor laughed. "Come on, Joy, I think you can come up with some realistic cuts if you honestly evaluate the situation. For instance: I'll bet you wash your hair every day of your life!"

Why had he said that? What did he mean? Was this a joke?

"No, I *don't* wash my hair every day. What's that got to do with high blood pressure?"

My doctor was still smiling. "I just thought you might be somewhat of a perfectionist, that's all. And perfectionism causes stress, you know.

"Well, here are some other things to work on. You need to get rid of salt and caffeine in your diet—and maybe a little weight. Do you have a regular exercise program?"

I thought I was going to cry, so I just shook my head.

"Exercise really doesn't do any good unless it's consistent, you know—three or four times a week. Daily is ideal, of course. Here's some literature for you to read. Now please, Joy, evaluate your stress level, for your own good. OK?"

"OK," I sighed. "Thank you."

Thanks for what? I was saying inside. On my way out of the office I caught sight of a woman with greasy hair. *Was I supposed to spend the rest of my life looking like that?*

In the next few months I made a definite effort to cut back on salt in my diet. As a matter of fact, everyone in my family forgot what salt looked or tasted like! If I couldn't have it, they didn't need it either! Fortunately, I'd never smoked, so nicotine wasn't a problem, but caffeine was. I began realizing how much I had used it for a "quick fix."

THE "SHOUTING SHOULDA'S"

Let's go back to my doctor's remarks about perfectionism. I had difficulty understanding his meaning because I didn't see myself as a perfectionist. To me, women whose houses were spotlessly clean were perfectionists; my house was never spotlessly clean, so I was *not* a perfectionist!

No, I didn't wash my hair every day, but I guess my doctor could tell that I was a little too concerned about what people thought of me. I *was* somewhat of a perfectionist in my expectations of myself.

Internally, I was always "shouting the shoulda's":

"I should get a full-time job to help with the finances."
"I shoulda' been more patient with the kids."
"I shoulda' been more sympathetic to my husband when he was home."
"I shoulda' spent more time on my Sunday school lesson and Bible study lesson."
"I should spend more time in Bible study and prayer."
"I should invite people over more than I do."

"I should get more involved in school and community activities."
"I should visit my neighbors more often to be a better witness."
"I shoulda' written letters to at least five people last week."
"I should clean up the messy areas in my house."

By the time I had screamed all my current "shoulda's," I was thoroughly debilitated. I felt like life's greatest failure. Then I started wondering if everyone realized all these negative things about me. Anxiety overwhelmed me as I questioned how God or anyone else could accept me "just as I am."

About this time the phone would ring and someone would ask me to take on another responsibility. My mind would reason frantically: *How can I say no when God might be speaking through this person?* Or perhaps I would run into someone who confirmed my suspicions about one of my problem areas. ("You never invite me to your house— guess you're just too busy playing the famous author!") In an effort to balance my life-style, I would end up overscheduling.

Later that year, my doctor advised me to resign from the teaching position I thought God had dropped into my lap. I felt like a total failure.

But my physical problems forced me to examine my way of living and, more important, my way of thinking! I had been living my life under a cloud of anxiety. I had recognized my insufficiency, but I had tried to keep it a secret. Now I had no choice but to lean on the all-sufficiency of El Shaddai. To trust Jehovah-jireh to supply my family's needs.

And to follow Jehovah-raah, the Good Shepherd, instead of relying on my own inadequate sense of direction.

JEHOVAH-RAAH, THE GOOD SHEPHERD

One of the opening phrases of the Twenty-third Psalm—"I shall not want"—took on a completely new meaning for me after I read Phillip Keller's delightful book, *A Shepherd*

Looks at Psalm 23. He pointed out that David, the author of the psalm, had experienced intense anguish and hardship while being pursued by his jealous father-in-law, King Saul. Therefore, it is absurd to assert that "sheep"—the children of God—will never experience lack or need.

Scriptures describe people like Ruth and Naomi, Elijah, John the Baptist, and many others who experienced times of overwhelming adversity. The Great Shepherd Himself, Keller stressed in his book, warned His disciples that in this world they would experience tribulation, but that they could "be of good cheer" because "I have overcome the world" (John 16:33, KJV).

What, then, is the meaning of the words "I shall not want?" Keller's definition is unique:

Since the Lord is my Shepherd, then I shall not want. Actually the word "want" as used here has a broader meaning than might at first be imagined. No doubt the main concept is that of not lacking—*not deficient*—in proper care, management, or husbandry.

But a second emphasis is the idea of being utterly contented *in the Good Shepherd's care and consequently not craving or desiring anything more. (Emphasis mine)*[1]

Formerly a sheep rancher, Keller vividly described a problem ewe he once owned. He came to call her "Mrs. Gadabout" because she was constantly on the lookout along the fences or shoreline for a loophole to crawl through. Often after she had forced her way through a weak or unprotected area, Keller would find her feeding on brown pasturage quite inferior to what he had carefully provided for her.

Despite his correction, she never learned her lesson. She continued to sigh over the so-called greener grass. Her discontentment affected not only her own behavior, but also the behavior of the other sheep, especially her lambs.

Keller further described "Mrs. Gadabout" in this way:

She was one of the most attractive sheep that ever belonged to me. Her body was beautifully proportioned. She had a strong constitution and an excellent coat of wool. Her head was clean, alert, well-set with bright eyes. She bore sturdy lambs that matured rapidly.

But in spite of all these attractive attributes, she had one pronounced fault. She was restless—discontented—a fence crawler. [2]

In her anxiety to find the best for herself and her family, Mrs. Gadabout defeated the shepherd's efficient efforts to care for her and her lambs.

Middle Eastern shepherds have a unique way of dealing with sheep who stray repeatedly. Sometimes the "Mrs. Gadabouts"—or the lambs who follow her—become so troublesome that a shepherd finds himself neglecting the other sheep on a regular basis to search for the wanderers. In cases like these, he will break the leg of the unteachable sheep to prevent further escape.

But that's not the end of the story! The shepherd binds up the broken leg and then tenderly carries the crippled lamb next to his heart until the leg is completely healed. By now the mature lamb has come to know and trust the compassionate heart of the shepherd.

The repentant King David referred to a similar experience of chastening after his sin with Bathsheba: "Make me to hear joy and gladness and be satisfied; let the bones which You have broken rejoice" (Ps. 51:8).

Only the Good Shepherd can bring joy out of devastation and brokenness.

A SHEPHERDESS AND THE SHEPHERD

When Biblical shepherds are mentioned, David usually comes to mind. And a Biblical shepherdess? Jacob's beloved Rachel.

Rachel was "shapely and in every way a beauty" (Gen.

29:17, TLB), in contrast to her sister Leah whose weak eyes may have been red and scaly in an allergic reaction to the desert sun. Perhaps, coming from the open fields, Rachel was unveiled when Jacob first saw her and emotionally kissed her. From that time on Rachel's whole world revolved around Jacob, her young god, and Jacob's whole world revolved around her.

I've always felt sorry for Leah, who stood by and watched while probably the most attractive man she had ever seen fell in love with her younger sister.

Jacob worked for Rachel's father, Laban, for seven years in order to win Rachel's hand. Those seven years seemed but a few days to Jacob because of his love. To Rachel, however, the tension-filled years of living with an unloved older sister probably seemed like forever. Rachel could hardly wait for the day when she could leave jealous Leah in her father's tent and begin a lifetime of perfect love!

But just as Jacob had tricked his father, Isaac, into giving him his brother Esau's birthright, so Jacob was tricked by his father-in-law, Laban. On what was to be Rachel's wedding night, Father Laban brought a heavily veiled Leah to a Jacob who may have celebrated too greatly with too much wine. The wedding was consummated, but with the wrong woman. Rachel and Leah were destined to share their lives as permanent points of an unhappy triangle.

And all three members of the triangle entered their emotional desert-wilderness. Jacob also received Rachel as a second wife, but the rivalry between the two sisters was intense. Later, in Leviticus 18:18, God ruled against one man marrying two sisters.

Rachel's early days as a shepherdess had probably been happy and carefree. In later days of anxiety, betrayal, and humiliation, however, Rachel may have begun to see her need of a spiritual Shepherd. Only Jehovah-raah could restore and satisfy her soul.

Poor Jacob could not endure her outbursts: "Give me children, or I'll die!" He said angrily, "Am I in the place of

God, who has kept you from having children?" Perhaps, to Rachel, he had been. So Jacob gave in to the alternative, the same one that Sarai had used years earlier—surrogate motherhood, this time through Rachel's handmaid, Bilhah.

Jacob was accustomed to the consequences of a woman's anxiety. He had lost home and family, including his relationship with his brother Esau, as a result of his mother's anxious manipulation.

Rachel's anxiety increased over the years, however, as her need for what then made a Jewish woman significant—a child—became greater and greater. The "shouting shoulda's" rang in her ears: "I should . . . I must . . . it is my responsibility to give Jacob a child!"

But her "shoulda's" were to no avail. Rachel's maid, Bilhah, gave two sons to Jacob. Rachel's sister, Leah, gave him four. Even Leah's maid contributed two more. Leah's daughter, Dinah, seemed a final leveling of the scales between the loved and lovely—and the unloved.

If Rachel could speak, perhaps this is what we would hear her say:

My mixed emotions were so complicated!
I loved you, Jacob, much too much to share
Your soul and body with my older sister . . .
And yet I knew she loved you just as much as I.
It hurt me as I watched her suffer.
It hurt me when you spent a night with her.
Unlike the games we played in childhood combat,
There was no winning in this adult tug-of-war!

And as our life went on, I found my pride was gone.
My beauty was no consolation when
I couldn't give you a son.
God taught us patience through those years of waiting
And gradually I learned to trust your God. [3]

Perhaps Rachel finally quit struggling to do that which she was unable to do. Perhaps she stopped screaming at

Jacob. It seems that when she recognized His Lordship, God began to work. He changed her body chemistry, and Rachel conceived a son. His name was Joseph. She died in childbirth with the second son, Benjamin.

Does God work the same way in every woman's life? Certainly not! God has created each one of us uniquely, and He has a unique plan for each of our lives. If you are unable to have children, He may have chosen you to give your love unselfishly to foster children. Or to serve as a teacher who has free time to give extra attention to her kids in school, time that a working mother wouldn't have. Or perhaps He is leaving your life open so that you can work or travel with your husband and be a blessing in some other unimagined way.

"He makes the barren woman to be . . . a joyful mother of [spiritual] children. Praise the Lord!" (Ps. 113:9).

How important it is that we look to the Shepherd for His special, individualized care!

Rachel's story of barren beauty is well-known in biblical history, but she is not unique in her frustration. I have lived with anxiety, and so have you. What is God saying to us in this story?

Rachel, the lovely shepherdess, understood the needs of sheep, one of the dumbest of all animals. She understood the responsibilities of raising and grazing creatures who will nibble themselves right off a mountainside, eat or drink things that are disastrous to their bodies, and literally live their lives in a rut if they are not led to new pastures. Sheep can easily lose their balance, roll over onto their backs, and freeze in place, unable to move on their own. She realized their need for protection from pests and parasites, from other animals—and, indeed, from themselves and their own stupidity.

Rachel must have recognized the helplessness of sheep without a shepherd. Before she saw her own need of a Shepherd, however, Rachel had to realize her own insufficiency.

Rachel's beauty could not compete with Leah's fertility.

Jacob's love could not fill the child-shaped vacuum in her life. Only Jehovah-raah could shepherd the shepherdess.

Dr. Lawrence J. Crabb comments:

Each of us has been programmed in his or her unconscious mind to believe that happiness, worth, joy—all the good things of life—depend upon something other than God. Our flesh (that innate disposition to oppose God) has responded happily to the world's false teaching that we are sufficient to ourselves, that we can figure a way to achieve true personal worth and social harmony without kneeling first at the cross of Christ. Satan has encouraged the development of a belief that we can meet our needs if only we had _____ . The blank is filled in differently, depending on one's particular temperament and family and cultural background. [4]

Rachel would have filled in the blank with the word *children*. At one time I would have written in: "enough money to put a down-payment on a house and pay off all our bills" or "a normal family life" (which would have involved my husband getting off the road). Time changes our answers.

What is your answer?

Anxiety is the fear that something I need will not be provided. What is the Good Shepherd's answer to your anxiety?

"You shall not want. . . ."

WHAT IS THE MEANING OF HIS NAME?

1. "I shall not want" (Ps. 23:1, KJV). According to Phillip Keller's definition, what are the main concepts expressed in the word "want"?

2. "He makes me to lie down . . ." (Ps. 23:1). Because of a sheep's makeup it is almost impossible for one to be made to lie down unless four requirements are met:

    a. It is free from fear.

    b. It is free from tension with other sheep.

    c. It is free from torment by flies or parasites.

    d. It is not hungry.

What are the equivalents in your life?

    a. What fear or anxiety is haunting you?

    b. What resentment against another person needs to be resolved?

    c. What "pests" (negative thoughts) are buzzing about your head?

    d. What is your greatest hunger?

Have you brought these problems to the Good Shepherd? Have you asked Him to restore your soul? Or are you busy looking for greener grass?

3. "He leads me beside the still waters" (Ps. 23:2). When sheep are led out to graze just before and after dawn, one of their main sources of water is the early morning dew. Happily refreshed, they can rest during the heat of the day. What parallels do you see between this fact and the Christian's quiet time?

4. "Yes, though I walk through the valley . . ." (Ps. 23:4). To avoid summer droughts, caring shepherds lead their sheep into mountain ranges, working their way up the mountains behind the snow line. The best route to the top, however, is always through the valleys, where streams can be found as well as the best forage. How can this view of the valleys in your life affect your attitude toward the Shepherd?

5. "Your rod and your staff, they comfort me" (Ps. 23:4). The shepherd's rod is a tool of power, authority, and defense, and therefore a comfort to the flock. How is the rod symbolic of the Word of God? Coming "under the rod" implies a thorough search of the sheep's wool and body for problems. For what problems does God our Shepherd search? Are you trying to "pull the wool over His eyes" in some area of your life?

6. A shepherd uses his staff to do the following: bring a newborn lamb to its mother's breast; bring the sheep close to himself for examination; guide and rescue the sheep. How are these roles paralleled in the work of the Holy Spirit?

7. "You anoint my head with oil" (Ps. 23:5). Summertime brings a rash of problems to the sheep, including the intensely irritating nose-flies, who lay their eggs on the damp mucous membranes of the sheep's nose. The larvae of the flies then work their way up the nasal passages into the sheep's head. Another problem is the highly contagious scab disease. Both of these aggravations were treated with oil. What is the Shepherd doing, then, when He anoints our heads with oil?

4

Why Is This World So Fragmented?

JEHOVAH-RAPHA:
The God who heals

Have you ever gone through an entire day without experiencing one negative thought or emotion?

I wonder if any of us has. These troubling interferences are facts of life.

If negative emotions are inevitable, can they be called sinful?

Obviously not. But some can lead us to sin. How do we recognize the turning point?

Try this line of demarcation. Any negative emotion that is counterproductive to compassion—blocking its development and exercise—is sin. And whenever the "bowels of compassion" (1 John 3:17, KJV) are blocked, we can become a "constipated Christian."[1]

Anyone who has experienced the lethargy and malaise associated with physical constipation can understand the parallel effects of spiritual constipation!

Take, for example, the influence of anxiety, which we discussed in the last chapter. Anxiety can range from legitimate concern to mind-ruling panic, an emotion that has completely lost sight of trust in a caring Shepherd. Panic also tends to block out feelings of concern for other sheep.

Resentment can be another cause of spiritual constipation. Although its effects are devastating, resentment can begin so subtly that Christians are often unaware of its presence until its later stages of development.

Certainly forgiveness is easier to verbalize—"Forgive us our debts as we forgive our debtors"—than to demonstrate. High expectations are regularly disappointed. Resentment takes the place of respect. We feel personally let down.

Disappointment, like resentment, can provoke spiritual constipation. One group of people who become the focal point of our high expectations are leaders and public figures—both Christian and non-Christian. The past decade has seen many Christian leaders topple and fall. Many times I have heard people ask: "How could he/she, whom I respected so highly, have done such a thing?" And another question may arise: "If this person, with his/her great knowledge of Scripture, couldn't resist temptation, how can I possible survive as a Christian?" Since the fallen leader represented God in the observer's mind, his failure may cause the observer to lose faith in God—or the capacity to trust future leaders.

After one personal disappointment of this kind, I received a letter from a spiritually mature friend who warned me against future pedestal-building. These were her helpful words:

This situation, along with many others I have encountered, once again points up to me that terrible danger of having our eyes on people—no matter who they are—making them our teachers rather than the Master-teacher, basing our lives on what they think rather than on the will of God which we have determined on our knees before Him with His Word.

I am also aware that I too can be deceived or am capable of deceiving myself. Many times the Holy Spirit reminds me, "Take heed when ye think ye stand, lest ye fall!" It is good for me, even though it shakes me up and hurts dreadfully, to know if and

*when a leader falls. There are people we do not even pray for
because we feel so confident that they have their act together and
we need never fear that they will err. These are all lessons for us.*

*I am often reminded when I speak at conferences and retreats
that God even spoke through an ass for Balaam.*

Mrs. Lois Ewald
Hephzibah House, New York City

"GREAT EXPECTATIONS"

For several reasons, family members (including in-laws!)
are often sources of irritation.

To begin with, we may expect certain things from God.
We may feel He owes us a complete family unit, a mom
and a dad "like everyone else's." Entire lives have been
ruined by resentment toward God because of a missing
parent.

Second, we may expect certain things from family
members. The physical presence of a parent does not
guarantee a good relationship with him or her. Yet we may
feel that our parents (or spouse or in-laws) should
instinctively understand our needs. Often these very
people, however, if they do exist, seem totally deaf, dumb,
and blind to our emotional needs. Perhaps they provide
well for our physical needs, or perhaps they feel no sense of
responsibility for us whatsoever.

Third, "forgiving and forgetting" is rough because we
simply cannot get away from family members! Even if my
problem person is not in my immediate family, I will still
see her eternally at holiday celebrations, weddings and
funerals. No matter how often I forgive her and even pray
for her, she may never change. She may keep right on
wounding me, beating me up emotionally.

It is easy to succumb to recurring attacks of "emotional
appendicitis." Even after the appendix—the core of
resentment that spreads the poison of bitterness through
the system—is gone, surgically removed by the Great

Physician, emotions may simulate the original symptoms out of force of habit.

At times like this I am learning to recognize the problem, rebuke Satan, and confess my renewed resentment.

Dr. Lawrence Crabb has helped me to deal with resentment by explaining that it comes from "believing that my needs are threatened by something which He (God) has allowed to happen to me."[2] The reminder that God is in control of every situation in my life because I have given myself totally to Him brings reassurance to the present and future rather than resentment against the people who seem to be blocking my path to happiness.

It also reminds me that what I may rationalize as justifiable resentment toward ornery people is actually a floating resentment toward the God who created them and allowed them to cross my path!

Think of resentment as a book you've checked out of the library and finished reading. You know what happens in the book. So don't renew it! Return it! Be honest with God in moments of struggle and tell Him that you don't seem to be able to control your emotions. It's your *will* He wants.

The following prayer may be helpful to you:

Lord, I want to please You in this relationship, but my emotions just aren't cooperating. I feel resentful toward _____ again. But that's only a feeling, a human emotion, a passing reaction. It's my will *You're concerned with, and my will is to please You. So I submit to You. I know Your will is for me to love that person as You love her. I don't feel capable of that today—in myself— but I do* will *not to dwell on my feelings of resentment toward her. And I am willing to allow You to make me willing to love her—someday.*

God can change emotions.

In His time.

I have met people who seem to actually enjoy the attention and sympathy they get when people realize what they have been through. Family problems can be used as crutches for so long that it becomes impossible to walk without them.

Resolving a past problem—not constantly rehashing and reliving it—is basic to coping with the present. Dealing with the present means taking responsibility for my actions and reactions, not blaming them on people from the past.

Bitterness binds us to the burdens of the past. Forgiveness releases us. It also unleashes our God-given creativity.

I have been privileged to witness this very process. Recently I received a letter written by a woman whose outlook on life was quite negative when we first met. Jane felt very much taken advantage of by her family. She had obvious potential in some areas, but was severely held back by what we thought was a lack of self-confidence. Her letter, however, revealed a lot more.

God has really been working on me as far as my past is concerned. He keeps bringing me to Philippians 3:13-14. Forgetting what lies behind and reaching for what lies ahead and reaching forward (my paraphrase), I have finally let go of the past. I have been able to let go of all the hurts and resentments . . . and I have come to accept my mom for who she is. I've started looking at what she has *done for me instead of what she has not.*

Now I find myself wanting to reach out and help others rather than waiting for them to make the first move. I feel like I have just been released from prison, and in a sense I guess I have.

Not only has my friend's negative outlook on life disappeared, but the creative energy that has been unleashed in her life is incredible! She has begun to travel, to take classes, to develop her gifts, and to use them in ministry. She is truly a new person.

The key statement in her letter is this: "I have come to accept my mom for who she is. I've started looking at what she *has* done for me instead of what she has not."

In one of the Psalms, David talked about expectations:

My soul, wait only upon God and silently submit to Him; for my hope and expectation are from Him.

Men of low degree . . . are emptiness—futility, a breath; and men of high degree are a lie and a delusion.

Power belongs to God. (Ps. 62:5, 9a, 11b)

A BIBLICAL FAMILY FEUD

Biblical families had problems too. The Bible is so valuable as a guide to life because it is so honest. Family problems are not omitted or glossed over.

The biblical story we will discuss in this chapter involved a sister, two brothers, and a sister-in-law who experienced some deep frustrations in dealing with each other. Sound familiar? The story of Moses, his wife Zipporah, and his brother Aaron and sister Miriam is essential to the understanding of another name of God—Jehovah-rapha.

In chapter 1 we discussed the righteousness and holiness and love implied in the name Jehovah. The name itself is derived from the Hebrew word *havah,* meaning "to be" or "being." Jehovah is the being who is completely self-existent, who has always existed, who is eternal and unchangeable.

In God's enigmatic answer to Moses' questions, "What shall I say to the Israelites? What is your name?" God said, "I AM WHO I AM and WHAT I AM, and I WILL BE WHAT I WILL BE" (Exod. 3:14).

God knew that even His highest creation—man—was capable of absorbing only a little knowledge of Him at a time.

I am the Lord.

I appeared to Abraham, to Isaac, and to Jacob, as God Almighty [El Shaddai], but by my name the Lord [Yahweh] [the redemptive name of God]—I did not make myself known to them. (Exod. 6:2-3)

Through compound names of Jehovah, however, God was beginning to reveal the fullness of His character to His people.

We are already familiar with the name of Jehovah-jireh, the God who provides for us just as He did for Abraham on Mount Moriah so many years ago. We have discussed the name of Jehovah-raah, the Good Shepherd who searches for us, chastens us when necessary, and holds us close to Himself during the healing process. In each compound name of Jehovah, there is a further revelation of God's ability to meet every need of His redeemed people.

And now, in Exodus 15, we encounter the name of Jehovah-rapha.

Led by Moses, the Hebrews had escaped from Egyptian bondage and crossed the Red Sea. Moses' sister, Miriam, was a central figure in this dramatic worship event. With timbrel in hand, the prophetess led the people in joyous praise: "Sing to the Lord, for He has triumphed gloriously and is highly exalted; the horse and his rider He has thrown into the sea" (Exod. 15:21).

During that day of sweet victory the Hebrews praised Jehovah, then continued their journey into the wilderness of Shur.

But "they went three days [33 miles] in the wilderness and found no water" (Exod. 15:22).

Perhaps their attitude of gratitude extended into the second day, but by the third day without water the people had forgotten Jehovah's might and mercy. Their parched throats voiced no paeons of praise, only caustic complaints.

Then, as they approached Marah, they saw a well. Can you imagine their jubilant rush to the watering place!

And when they came to Marah, they could not drink of the waters of Marah, for they were bitter: therefore the name of it was called Marah [which means bitter].

And the people murmured against Moses, saying, What shall we drink?

And he cried unto the Lord; and the Lord showed him a tree, which when he had cast into the waters, the waters were made sweet: there he made for them a statute and an ordinance, and there he proved them, And said, If thou wilt diligently hearken to the voice of the Lord thy God, and wilt do that which is right in his sight, and wilt give ear to his commandments, and keep all his statutes, I will put none of these diseases upon thee, which I have brought upon the Egyptians: for I am the Lord that healeth thee. (Exod. 15:23-26, KJV)

Jehovah-rapha means "Jehovah heals." Does that promise apply only to physical needs?

The medicinal tree that God directed Moses to cast into the water is a type or forerunner of another tree. A tree that also stretched its arms to the sky. A tree that was cut down to become part of a greater Sacrifice.

That Sacrifice was Jesus Christ, the remedy for our Marah, our bitterness. The tree was the cross.

But wanderers in the wilderness witnessed only one miracle, the healing of the waters. Their attitudes, however, were not healed. Soon they went back to murmuring against the Lord—and their leader, Moses.

Where was Miriam? What was her attitude during this time? Did she stand by Moses, supporting him spiritually and emotionally as she had protected him physically years earlier? Probably she did, encouraging him as she encouraged loyalty in her people.

But something happened in this brother-sister relationship. In Numbers 12 another woman, Moses' wife, entered the picture. Perhaps Zipporah, Moses' Midianite wife, had died and Moses had remarried. The Bible tells us that Miriam and Aaron criticized Moses because of his choice.

Miriam may have felt jealous of this intruder and her influence. Perhaps she said something like this:

Why did she *come into our lives?*
Why does he need a woman? Why?
Did marriage work for him before?
Can't God fulfill his every need?
My *love's for Israel and our God*
Who's chosen Moses . . . Aaron . . . me.
Our unity of spirit's gone;
She's torn apart our family![3]

Miriam, in her unhappiness, had developed a critical spirit. It seems she passed it on to brother Aaron. God, in His holiness, would not allow this unfair treatment of His faithful servant.

The sudden blanching of Miriam's olive-colored skin pinpointed God's indignation:

The Lord said to Moses, Aaron, and Miriam . . . Hear now My words: If there is a prophet among you, I the Lord make Myself known to him in a vision, and speak to him in a dream.

But not so with My servant Moses; he is entrusted and faithful in all My house.

With him I speak mouth to mouth [directly] clearly and not in dark speeches; and he beholds the form of the Lord. Why then were you not afraid to speak against My servant Moses?

And when the cloud departed from over the tent . . . Miriam was leprous, as white as snow. (Num. 12:4, 6-8, 10)

Miriam's sin was made very clear to all Israel in her week-long exile from the camp. The outward "uncleanness" of leprosy was symbolic of a greater need for inner cleansing.

It is significant that Moses, the brother Miriam had criticized, was the one who cried out to God for her healing. Moses' prayer was answered. After seven days Miriam was restored, physically and spiritually.

Restored by Jehovah-rapha, the God who heals.

This dramatic but down-to-earth story shows the

importance of allowing God to do the judging. He doesn't need "Monday morning quarterbacks"!

As Miriam learned so abruptly, God sees bitterness toward a brother as bitterness toward Himself, the God who created—and loves—that brother!

Today, if you will hear [the Holy Spirit's] voice,

Do not harden your hearts, as [happened] in the rebellion [of Israel] and their provocation and embitterment [of Me] in the day of testing in the wilderness,

Where your fathers tried [My patience] and tested [My forbearance] and found I stood their test. . . .

And so I was provoked (displeased and sorely grieved) with that generation, and said, They always err and are led astray in their hearts, and they have not perceived or recognized My ways and become progressively better and more experimentally and intimately acquainted with them *(emphasis mine).*

So we see that they were not able to enter [into His rest] because of their unwillingness to adhere to and trust and rely on God—unbelief had shut them out. (Heb. 3:7-10, 19)

Jehovah's continuous revelation of Himself and His ways fell upon deaf ears in the wilderness.

In our wildernesses, are we listening to the voice of God? Or are our ears filled with the sounds of our bitter complaints? Can we enter into rest?

Jehovah-rapha points to the tree that will make the bitter waters sweet. Only the cross of Jesus can make the difference.

WHAT IS THE MEANING OF HIS NAME?

Retrospection. 1. We often overreact to a situation when we have not properly handled a hurt or other stress from the past. Think back to times when you failed to express your feelings, either because there was no one to talk to or because you were too afraid or ashamed to tell anyone. Can you see the relation between those times and later times when you overreacted to routine problems—or reacted bitterly to another's happiness—without understanding why you felt the way you did? How do you feel after you overreact?

2. Sooner or later, like Miriam, most people either express or explode, whether outwardly or inwardly. When negative emotions are not expressed in constructive ways, they resemble the poison from a ruptured appendix that infects the entire body. What does Hebrews 12:15 say about resentment and its big brother bitterness?

3. In *Healing for Damaged Emotions,* David A. Seamands said, "Grace is the face God wears when He looks at us in all our shortcomings and failures." Take time now to follow the counsel of Hebrews 4:16 and approach God's "throne of grace" to "obtain mercy and find grace to help in time of need" (KJV). Ask Jehovah-rapha to search your heart and pinpoint people toward whom you feel resentment. Resolve to ask forgiveness where necessary. (At one time I had a list of seventeen people!)

Relaxation. Read the following statement aloud to help you relax in the love of Jehovah-rapha: "As I confessed my resentment toward people and toward God, Jesus interceded for me and God the Father forgave me. I am accepted in the Beloved (Eph. 1:6). I am in His presence. His Holy Spirit comforts me. I am loved."

Re-creation of Spirit* (Warm-up Exercises).

1. Front and Center: Face problems squarely.
Plan a strategy for dealing with resentment. Should you make yourself accountable to someone else on a regular

*See Psalm 51:1.

basis? Why is it often so hard to share honestly with others how you feel? If you need to confide in someone, what kind of person do you go to? Are you the kind of person another might choose?

2. Stretch to the Right: Face responsibilities.
What is the danger in passing the blame for our feelings onto others? Why is this practice usually self-defeating? How do we harden our hearts against God? (See Heb. 3:8.)

3. Long Look Inside: Determine to be healed.
Is it possible that some people really do not want to be healed of resentment? Why? What might they really want?

4. Stretch to the Left: Forgive those involved.
Why is it so hard to forgive? What did Jesus say about forgiving others? How is forgiving others a way of taking responsibility for yourself? How was the cross the ultimate symbol of forgiveness?

5. Lean Back: Forgive yourself.
Why is it a contradiction to say that you believe Jehovah-rapha forgives you but you cannot forgive yourself? Why is forgiving oneself so important? What happens to a person who never forgives himself for past mistakes or sins?

6. Look Up: There's a Hand reaching down!
What is the role of the Holy Spirit in relation to our prayers? (See Rom. 8:26.) Why do we need the Spirit's help in prayer? How can the Spirit help us pinpoint our problems? (See Ps. 139:23-24.)

5

Why Did God Allow This to Happen?

ADONAI:
Lord and Master
ISHI: Husband

The theme of the retreat at which I was preparing to speak was joy. Then why did I feel drawn to an Old Testament story of desire, adultery, murder, and cover-up? Weren't there more uplifting, joyful topics?

But the joy mentioned in Psalm 51, the psalm that David wrote as his confession of sin with Bathsheba, kept prodding me in the direction of the story told in 2 Samuel 11. David's joy, the joy of restoration, had been preceded by the brokenness of repentance.

David emphasized this fact in Psalm 32:3-5:

When I kept silence [before I confessed], my bones wasted away through my groaning all the day long. For day and night Your hand [of displeasure] was heavy upon me; my moisture was turned into the drought of summer. . . . I acknowledged my sin to You, and my inquity I did not hide. I said, I will confess my transgressions to the Lord [continually unfolding the past till all is told], then You [instantly] forgave me the guilt and iniquity of my sin. Selah [pause, and calmly think of that]!

God spoke to me clearly through His Word: "Put pride aside! Share what you have learned!"

God had been teaching me to recognize and confront my negative emotions. For years I had succumbed to anxiety—fear that God would not supply my needs, whether physical, spiritual, or emotional. I had also lost round after round to resentment—the belief that my needs were threatened by something God had allowed in my life.

And then there was lust. Lust urges us to go outside of God's will to get what we think we need. Its variations are power-lust, greed-lust, popularity-lust, and pleasure-lust, as well as sex-lust. Guilt is the result of giving in to lust, whether in thoughts or in actions.

Anxiety, resentment, and guilt—each little EMO (negative emotion) has the ability to creep up on us so slyly and subtly that we fail to recognize its presence. Suddenly it dominates our thought processes! Instead of bringing each thought into captivity to the obedience of Christ (2 Cor. 10:5), we allow negative emotions to become Satan's strongholds.

For years I had regretted my captivity to negative emotions, but felt helpless to break the EMO cycle.

Remorse is merely another emotion. Repentance, however, as outlined in Psalm 32, is obedience to God's voice.

In order to break my EMO cycle, God took me, like David, through a time of repentance and confession—in my case, with the help of chicken pox! As I shared in chapter 1, He created in me a clean heart; He renewed a right spirit within me; He restored to me the joy of His salvation (Ps. 51:10-12).

Now, as I prepared for the retreat, God showed me He was fulfilling Psalm 51:13: "Then will I teach transgressors Your ways, and sinners shall be converted and return to You."

I stopped arguing with God. There must be someone at that retreat who needed to hear the story of Bathsheba. I

packed a royal blue dress, trimmed in gold braid, that I had
bought in Israel, to better play the part of a soldier's-wife-
turned-queen.

LINDA: A CONTEMPORARY BATHSHEBA

The Bible is very clear concerning David's actions toward
Bathsheba, but I have often wondered about Bathsheba's
response. Did she feel there was no choice involved when
the king called for her? Or was David's passion returned by
this wife of an absentee soldier?

On Saturday evening of the weekend retreat, wearing
the blue dress, I presented the possibility that Bathsheba
had battled anxiety and resentment toward her husband's
busy life-style, finally succumbing to sexual lust and the
resulting guilt.

I wanted him to see me . . . yes, it's true.
Perhaps I wouldn't admit it—
Even to myself—
But as I watched that regal body dance before the Lord,
I thought of what it would be like to be his queen.
And when Uriah left for war,
I asked if David too had gone.

And so that evening when I bathed,
I realized he could see.
The call came quickly, quietly:
"Come to the king."
I went.
I didn't have to ask the reason for his call.
I read it in his eyes.

I am with child.
I can't believe that this is happening to me.
Yet here I am, Uriah's wife,
With David's child inside my womb.
Have I gone mad?

What will I do?
What can I do?
I need Uriah's loyal arms![1]

God's Word convicted of sin. His Spirit worked in hearts. To my amazement, when the altar call was given, about a dozen women knelt at the rustic tabernacle altar and sobbed out their confessions.

A slim girl in blue jeans and French braids came to me later, quietly. "May I talk to you for a few minutes?"

We sat down on an old wooden bench. I noticed that her eye makeup was smeared and tried to guess her age. Maybe nineteen? Twenty-one?

She finally spoke. "My name's Linda. I don't know why I came. I've never been to a retreat before. I didn't know anyone here. But somehow I felt compelled to get on that bus and come. I really didn't know why."

Her voice quivered. "But when you talked about Bathsheba and David tonight, I found out why. I've been separated from my husband for a month and I've lost my job because . . . because. . . ."

"You were involved with someone at work, Linda, is that it?"

"Yes. And now I've lost my job and he's lost his because of me, and I'm losing my marriage—but we can't stay away from each other! We still see each other at school. Tonight . . . tonight I knew it was wrong."

I spoke gently. "That's a good start, Linda. But that's not enough. I think you realize that you have to break it off. You have to stop seeing him completely. As long as you're still seeing him, you won't forget him. It may feel like love, but real love doesn't hurt other people or break God's laws."

Linda's eyes were full of tears. "That prayer you read tonight—could I have a copy of it?"

That evening I had explained that when people become unnaturally bonded to each other in a sinful relationship, they become helpless to control their emotions or their actions.

How to deal with this? The Bible tells us in Psalms 32 and 51 (written by one who had experienced it firsthand!) that the mind must be cleansed by confession of sin and then occupied by right thinking. If it's not, "the final condition . . . is worse than the first," Jesus warned (Matt. 12:45, NIV). The patterns of wrong thinking can become so indelibly engraved on the mind that only the two-edged cutting blade of God's Word can root them out, and only the seed of His promises can bring new life.

An article written by Karen Mains offered a forceful word picture of how to deal with an unnatural relationship, a passion fueled by the lustful spirit of our age that seems totally out of control. Karen suggests that it is helpful to close the eyes in prayer and picture the One who is stronger than this bondage, the One who is able to loose all bonds.

He is described by the Apostle John in Revelation 1:13-16 (TLB):

. . . *the Son of Man, wearing a long robe circled with a golden band across his chest. His hair was white as wool or snow, and his eyes penetrated like flames of fire. His feet gleamed like burnished bronze, and his voice thundered like the waves against the shore. He held seven stars in his right hand and a sharp, double-edged sword. . . .*

Linda had requested the prayer from Karen's article:

"Lord, I have sinned against you and against my fellow man. I have committed adultery either in my mind or in my body. I repent. I am sorry. I confess my sin. Forgive me."

In your mind see three people. See yourself and the one to whom you are unnaturally bound. See the cords of bondage that bind you together. Now see Christ. See this One who loves you. He stands between you and the other for whom you have carried

*an unnatural affection. Christ holds a flaming sword in His
hand. It is the sword of the Spirit, the spirit of truth.*

*He takes that sword and severs the cords of bondage. He cuts
the cords in two. Christ has broken the bonds. In your mind see
the person to whom you were bound turn his or her back to you,
and you turn to Christ and allow Him to open His arms and
receive you unto Himself.*

*This prayer tool is a powerful aid in visualizing Christ's
freedom in the interpersonal bondages of our lives. You may have
to pray it again and again until you experience release. But
release will come.²*

I gave Linda my copy of the "prayer of severing," asking
her to return it to me the next morning at breakfast. The
tear-stained article was returned, but I don't remember
ever seeing Linda again. I don't even know her last name.
All I am able to do, as the Lord reminds me, is to pray that
she is enclosed in His loving embrace.

At breakfast that next morning several notes were
handed to me. The first one reminded me that "weeping
may endure for a night, but joy cometh in the morning"
(Ps. 30:5, KJV). Another: "The joy of the Lord is your
strength" (Neh. 8:10, KJV).

God had rewarded my obedience to Him with joy.

"NO ONE WANTS TO DIRTY THEIR HANDS . . ."
My friend Linda had never attended a retreat before the
one in Oregon, at which I spoke. Since the story of David
and Bathsheba seemed new to her, probably she had not
been a regular church attender. Evidently someone,
however, had cared enough about her to invite her—
perhaps someone like the writer of the letter I received
several weeks after the retreat.

*So often people want to forget and push away the Bathshebas of
life. No one wants to dirty their hands, but we can be used of
God to see past the dirt and filth to the value of lost souls. As*

*wrong as they are, their problems certainly are real. There are
thousands of those waiting for a* loving *call to repentance,
without condemnation, to a life of security and health in the
bosom of Jesus. It is such a lonely existence with a future of
nothingness that they possess.*

*There are too many "Christians" who do not want to get
involved to help the wayward return. People just don't want to
mess with the messy. Praise God,* He *is faithful! Thanks for being
bold enough to stand and soft enough to call.*

Bathshebas, however, are not only outside the church.
At another retreat I spoke with Elaine, a beautiful young
mother who had been involved in an emotionally—not
physically—adulterous relationship with a church leader.
Elaine reconfirmed my conviction that the story of
Bathsheba has a far-reaching message.

Dear Joy,

*It feels a little strange tonight, reflecting upon the weekend
that, last evening, had me soaring with thanksgiving. EMO is
begging me to please relax and get back to the securities of the
familiar, the easy, the not-so-flesh-threatening thoughts of my
life. In a very real way I need to write to you, to affirm for myself
what God is doing . . . to touch base with this relative stranger
to whom I spilled my guts yesterday!*

*Part of me is appalled at having taken the risk in confessing
all I did. The other part feels—or rather knows—that a member
of Christ's Body has been instrumental in transmitting another
outpouring of fresh oil in this process of restoration and healing.
I am truly thankful for your obedience in sharing with us what
you did.*

*When you concluded with the comment about Bathsheba
being privileged to be part of the lineage of Christ, I believe our
precious Father put the finishing touch on His assurance to me of
His forgiveness, understanding, and love.*

I have not yet, in this painful year, experienced so much

freedom. I am absolutely in awe of God's doings. And to think I
was so close to declining the invitation to go to the retreat.

Love in Jesus,
Elaine

Elaine's experience scarred her life, but its aftereffects do
not compare to the emotional crippling that may result
from a physically adulterous relationship.

June, a lovely middle-aged woman I met at another
retreat, told me that her story was living proof of 1
Corinthians 6:18 (TLB): ". . . run from sex sin. No other sin
affects the body as this one does. When you sin this sin it is
against your own body."

June had confessed her adultery to God and to her
husband, taking full responsibility for what had happened,
but she couldn't seem to forgive herself—or her husband—
for allowing it to happen.

I asked June if she was still holding on to any reminders
of the affair. She admitted that she still had several shirts in
her closet that had belonged to her former lover. We
decided they had to go. She also mentioned that she still
had a key to the man's place of business; I advised her to
get rid of it.

The next morning June handed the key to a friend of
mine with these words: "Joy will know what this is."
Although she had not communicated with her former lover
in two years, this symbol of her "place of refuge" had
waited in her purse, ever-ready for use.

Later, an understanding woman counselor encouraged
June to write a letter to her husband so that he could
understand his responsibility to help pick up the pieces of
their marriage. The affair was now two years in the past,
but June was surprised at how vivid her memories of it
were. She has given me permission to use her letter.

Dear husband,
I never thought I would become involved in an affair. Not
me—the spiritual one! The mother whose kids were always in

Sunday school, who regularly attended prayer meeting as well as Sunday services.

Certainly I never thought of becoming involved with him! *You remember I never liked the man, never trusted him all those years I had known him, was wary of his flowery compliments and praise. I had heard things about him and other women, and I would show him that at least one woman was not susceptible to his charms! Probably that was why you, my husband, thought nothing of my going to work for him.*

He knew my standards, I felt sure, and I would have no problems. I had no idea that as I got to know him, my respect for his intelligence would greatly increase. The man was much more interesting than I had realized. He knew how to bring out the best in other people by finding their unique strengths and abilities, encouraging them, and praising what they had accomplished.

It was rewarding to have a boss so appreciative of my abilities. Especially when you, my husband, seemed to take me so much for granted. Of course, we had been married almost fifteen years. . . .

At our house it seemed as though I had to fulfill everyone's needs. It was nice to have someone aware of my *needs for a change. Just insignificant little things. Like the day I mentioned that I needed a good dictionary. The next day an expensive, new Unabridged was lying on my desk. Just a gift from the boss, who was becoming a friend.*

And then there was the day my hayfever got the best of me. My boss looked at me with concern and said, "Why don't you go to an allergist? Here . . . I'll give you the name and phone number where I go." He understood how miserable I felt. Just that morning you had made a joke about owning shares in the Kleenex corporation. I didn't think it was funny.

Our conversations—if you could call them that—were becoming more and more a series of backlashes, of sarcastic comments on what the other had said. If, indeed, there was any comment at all. Often, when I tried to discuss something important to me, you said nothing. I wondered if you had even heard me.

My boss, on the other hand, began to rely on me as a

sounding board for his ideas. Once he said I provided impetus for his creativity. I became aware of an intellectual stimulation when we exchanged ideas.

Then it happened! One day my boss told me of a spiritual renewal in his life. He was tired of living the way he had for so many years, he said, thinking only of his own desires and needs. He wanted to dedicate his life to the Lord, and he thanked me for being a part of this new adventure. I was caught off guard by his humility and honesty. I felt a new kinship with him.

Tragically, I had looked, prayed, and even asked for spiritual leadership from you but, it seemed, to no avail. Our times of spiritual communion had always been sporadic and unsatisfying. The tyranny of the urgent—the business, the phone, the doorbell—had always taken precedence over my needs.

I never thought I would become involved in an affair . . . but I did.

Can you help me insure that it will never happen again?

Your wife,
June

The problems within June's marriage had developed over a long period of time. The third party was not the key factor involved; this was an affair "just waiting to happen."

June and her husband experienced several years of agony, but they chose to let it draw them closer together. After confession to God and to each other, they continued to communicate with each other. In time, both were able to forgive each other and themselves and to receive and feel forgiveness from God.

In His time . . .

A caring counselor who refused to be shocked by June's past was the catalyst God used to help June take the final step in the healing process.

GOMER'S GETAWAY

As you read this, you too may be dealing with pressures you cannot admit to or confide in anyone. Perhaps you can identify with one of the women in this chapter. Perhaps you are—or were—married to someone who seemed to be married only to his work and/or his church, and you struggle with feelings of bitterness toward God as well as your spouse.

Perhaps your screams sound like those of Gomer, runaway wife of the Old Testament prophet Hosea:

How can I go back?
A prophet's wife must be above reproach,
And I'm below the lowest.
Can I tell him
I felt his standards were too high
Right from the start?
Those righteous-looking people
Who hang upon each word he speaks
Look down on me.
I couldn't play the role.
They wondered all along
Why such a man chose me.
So to escape from righteous stares,
The pain of worthlessness,
I left for other worlds
Where I could cope with life,
Where little was expected of me,
Where I could be myself.[3]

Hosea watched his wife as she visited lover after lover, as one man after another used her. And abused her.

Then Hosea, at God's direction, bargained at the slave block to redeem a prostitute—his own unfaithful wife.

And now Hosea's bought me back!
He says he loves me
Just as God loves Israel
With an everlasting love . . .
I just don't understand.[4]

We humans can take revenge in stride, but we find it hard to understand grace. Dr. David Seamands has defined it well: "Grace is the face God wears when He meets our imperfection, sin, weakness, and failure. Grace is what God is and what God does when he meets the sinful and undeserving."[5]

God showed the tenderness of His heart through Hosea:

I will speak tenderly and to her heart.
   There I will . . . make the Valley of Achor or Troubling to be for her a door of hope and expectation. And she shall sing there and respond as in the days of her youth. . . .
   And it shall be in that day, says the Lord, that you will call me Ishi *or My Husband, and you shall call Me no more Baali or My Baal. (Hos. 2:14-16, emphasis mine)*

What a sensitively drawn picture of God's love for the nation of Israel and also for His Bride, the Church! God is saying that even though He has created and then bought back His Bride at the auction block, she is not to think of Him as her *Baal* (owner or possessor) but as *Ishi,* the most loving of husbands.

God understood
He knew her fickle heart,
Her hurts and hang-ups.
He also knew His power
Could change her life
If she would let Him heal her hurts
Resolve her hang-ups
And renew her heart.[6]

HEALING THE HURT
Your situation may be completely different from Gomer, Hosea's unfaithful wife. Perhaps the situation was reversed: Your husband or boyfriend was unfaithful to you.

Or perhaps you feel rejected because there is no one in your life. The loneliness is a deep hurt.

As mentioned earlier, the Hebrew word *Ishi* is used in a very special way to picture God's love and concern. After my mother's death, I found this passage heavily underlined in my mother's worn Bible.

Sing, O barren, you who did not bear; break forth into singing and cry aloud, you who did not travail with child! For the [spiritual] children of the desolate one will be more than the children of the married wife. . . .

Enlarge the place of your tent, and let the curtains of your habitations be stretched out; spare not, lengthen your cords and strengthen your stakes. . . .

Fear not, for you shall not be ashamed; neither be confounded and depressed, for you shall not be put to shame; for you shall forget the shame of your youth, and you shall not [seriously] remember the reproach of your widowhood any more.

For your Maker is your husband [Ishi], *the Lord of hosts is His name; and the Holy One of Israel is your Redeemer, the God of the whole earth He is called.*

For the Lord has called you like a woman forsaken, grieved in spirit and heartsore, even a wife [wooed and won] in youth, when she is later refused and scorned, says your God.

For a brief moment I forsook you, but with great compassion and mercies I gather you to Me again.

In a little burst of wrath I hid My face from you for a moment, but with age-enduring love and kindness I will have compassion and mercy on you, says the Lord, your Redeemer. (Isa. 54:1-2, 4-7, emphasis mine)

After experiencing a life-altering rejection, how do we "enlarge the place of our tents" when everything within us wants to shrink from public view and contract into numbness? How do we become healed helpers? How do we turn miseries into ministries?

A dear friend answered that question. She listed the

stages she experienced in recovery from the poignant hurt of rejection and unfaithfulness:

1. *Numbness*
2. *Unreality ("This can't be happening to me . . . this is a bad dream and I'll wake up!")*
3. *Emotional hurt*
4. *Tears*
5. *Resentment (directed toward God and people)*
6. *Decision: Will this draw me closer to or away from God?*
7. *Forgiving (freely, fully, forgetfully—"even as God for Christ's sake has forgiven you")*
8. *Healing of scabs and scars (A slow process. Chuck Swindoll said, "Sometimes when you're alone the past slips from behind like a freak ocean wave and overwhelms you. The scab is jarred loose, the wound stays inflamed and tender, and you wonder if it will ever go away.")*
9. *Praying for strength from the Holy Spirit (hour by hour if necessary, to give peace and calmness and to ease the pain)*
10. *Trusting Christ with my day (the same trust I once placed in Him when I asked Him to save me and now place in Him whenever I ask for cleansing)*

And so in this chapter we see two pictures of God.

Gomer's *Ishi* (husband), the unconditionally loving Hosea, is an Old Testament image of Jesus Christ who said: "Let him who is without sin among you be the first to throw a stone . . ." (John 8:7).

Another picture of God is the awesome Son of Man described in the first chapter of Revelation, whose flame-like vision penetrates our hearts. His snow-white purity is in sharp contrast to our middle-of-the-road tolerance. His thundering voice convicts of sin. His double-edged sword severs wrong affections and relationships.

He is our Adonai.

MY ADONAI, LORD AND MASTER

At one time I found it difficult to understand how King David—an adulterer, murderer, and cover-up artist—could have been called "a man after God's own heart."

I also looked at other people's mistakes and said: "Something like that could never happen to me."

I've learned to say: "There, but for the grace of God, go I. . . ."

David began his kingship with a humble heart, a heart that yearned after God. In an attitude of complete submission, he frequently used the word "Adonai"—Lord of lords, Master of masters; he called himself God's servant.

Our understanding of the master-servant relationship is negatively influenced by pre-Civil War history, but David understood the Old Testament concept. A master was responsible to protect, advise, and care for his servant; a servant, although he owed his master unrestricted obedience and service, was even eligible to inherit the estate of a childless master.

In 2 Samuel 7:18-20 the words "Lord God" appear four times in three verses, as David responded to Adonai's promise to establish his kingdom forever:

Who am I, O Lord God [Adonai], and what is my house, that You have brought me this far? Then as if this were a little thing in Your eyes, O Lord God [Adonai], You have spoken also of Your servant's house in the far distant future. . . . What more can David say to You? For You know Your servant, Lord God [Adonai]. (Brackets mine)

In this conversation with God, David remembered his humble origins as a shepherd boy. At this point in his life it may have been difficult for David to imagine himself in a situation where he would murder a man to cover his own adultery.

At this point he probably would have said: "Something like that could never happen to me."

The following warning emphasizes the need for accountability to our Adonai:

It must be stressed that obedience does not automatically follow from correct understanding. . . . It often involves teeth-gritting effort to choose to behave as we should. . . . Apart from the clear exercise of the will, there will be no consistent obedience. As the Christian continues to choose the path of righteousness, his capacity for right choices in the face of adversity and temptation enlarges. He becomes a stronger Christian, one whom God can trust with greater responsibilities. [7]

Remember: God's opinion of sexual sin does not change with the passing of time. "Sexual sin is never right: our bodies were not made for that, but for the Lord, and the Lord wants to fill our bodies with himself" (1 Cor. 6:13b, TLB).

WHAT IS THE MEANING OF HIS NAME?

1. Is choosing Jesus Christ as Adonai an emotional reaction or an act of the will?

2. Dr. Lawrence Crabb made the following observation:

Preachers and counselors can spend their energy exhorting people to change their behavior. But human will is not a free entity. It is bound to a person's understanding. . . . When a person understands *who Christ is, on what basis he is worthwhile, and what life is all about, he has the formulation necessary for any sustained change in life-style. Christians who try to "live right" without correcting a wrong understanding about how to meet personal needs will always labor and struggle with Christianity, grinding out their responsible duty in a joyless, strained fashion.*

Christ taught that when we know the truth, we can be set free. We now are free *to choose the life of obedience because we understand that in Christ we are worthwhile persons. We are free to express our gratitude in the worship and service of the One who has met our needs.*[8]

In light of the above passage, discuss the difference between legalism and the obedience that results from understanding.

3. In Exodus 4:10, Moses used the word *Adonai* while trying to evade God's commission to deliver Israel. Why was God's anger kindled against him? (See Exod. 4:11-13.)

4. Jeremiah, as well as Moses, was filled with feelings of inadequacy when God called him to speak. (See Jer. 1:6.) How did God respond to this prophet's protest? (See Jer. 1:7-10.)

5. How does Romans 12:1 express what our response should be to our Adonai?

6. Adam was tempted in a beautiful garden where he lacked nothing, and he succumbed. His disobedience cost him everything. (See Gen. 3.) Jesus was tempted in a barren wilderness; miserably alone and hungry almost to the point of starvation, He resisted. Obedience to His heavenly Father brought Jesus into a closer relationship with Him. (See Luke 4:1-14.) Later, the Apostle Paul spent time in the deserts of Arabia in preparation for service. (See Gal. 1:16-17.) What can happen when we deliberately bypass the desert experiences? Does one successful resistance mean that we are impervious to future attacks? (See Luke 4:13.)

7. What point does Paul make in Romans 6:16?

8. In Jeremiah 46:10 a "day of Adonai" is mentioned. How is it described?

9. What words can those of us who know Jesus Christ as

Adonai look forward to hearing someday? (See Matt. 25:21.)

10. In Isaiah 6:1-8, read the prophet's description of his vision of God as Adonai. In the light of this passage, bow in the presence of your Adonai, your Lord and Master. Draw near to Him with adoration; worship Him. In honesty and humility, confess your sins. Give thanks for His forgiveness, His great goodness. Then, and only then, bring supplications to His Majesty.

6

I'm Out of Control!

JEHOVAH-SABAOTH:
The Lord of Hosts

King David might never have confessed his sin with Bathsheba had it not been for a man who was willing to confront him and hold him accountable for his sin. Nathan the prophet pointed the stern finger of truth at a powerful king and delivered God's message: "Thou art the man!"

Nathan risked his life for the sake of accountability. In our day, however, the need for accountability is often a neglected truth. It needs to be preached from every pulpit.

Yet as important as accountability is, there are times when we need another truth emphasized—the truth of acceptability.

Dr. Lawrence Crabb comments:

If I understand accountability, but not acceptability, I will live under pressure to behave well in order to be accepted. If I understand acceptability, but not accountability, I may become casually indifferent to sinful living. When I understand first my acceptability and then my accountability, I will be constrained to please the One who died for me, fearful that I might grieve Him, not wanting to, because I love Him.

True significance and security are available only to the Christian, one who is trusting in Christ's perfect life and substitutionary death as his sole basis of acceptability before a holy God. [1]

Sadly, many Christians still experience feelings of insignificance even though they *are* "trusting in Christ's perfect life and substitutionary death." Head knowledge is not heart acknowledgment. How do we come to a full realization of what it means to be "accepted in the Beloved" (Eph. 1:6, KJV)?

In the past three chapters we discussed the "fearsome threesome"—anxiety, resentment, and guilt. These three negative emotions can subtly begin to dominate our thought processes and reactions and eventually determine our attitudes and actions. They are particularly dangerous because God did not plan or create our physical bodies to coexist with them on a permanent basis.

When anxiety, resentment, and guilt constantly interact with the body processes, the body's resistance to disease is broken down. As a result, we become physically as well as emotionally vulnerable.

And our reactions to other people, even our best friends, may become extremely negative. We find ourselves feeling and saying things that just aren't typical of the good-humored person who lives at our house.

Eventually we get really "down" on ourselves, as Penny did.

Penny is the fictitious name of a loving, likeable, and gifted young woman. She is intelligent, organized, and efficient—and has a great sense of humor as well. But at times Penny does not feel accepted or acceptable. The following letter is evidence.

Here we go again. Another get-together where I'll slowly wilt into the background and she'll *become the focus of attention. Did you ever feel there was one person who seemed to be especially bestowed with a winning personality and a life with most of the big questions answered? That's what Hannah seems like. She has such a bubbly personality. She's the life of every party. She's the type that everybody hugs.*

Hannah has so many talents. She can cook and sew and cross-

stitch. She can play two instruments. She's the person everybody can confide in—students, girls in the youth group, etc.

Not only does she have a winning personality, but it's like God must have a special cup of blessing with her name on it. A cup that is larger than anyone else's.

First He calls her to a special vocation. He gives her a clear, undoubtable call. So off to college. She is able to focus her studies around her call, giving them a special significance, a special motivation.

I'm not so blessed. Temporarily working at a job that offers no challenge, I go to college for different reasons. First, it was always something I'd wanted to do—and maybe while I was there I'd sense God's direction for my life.

At school Hannah's personality won her many friends. People were always in her room or sitting beside her at mealtimes. Hannah would show me all the letters and cards she received. The whole time I was there I think I got two cards.

I don't warm up to people very quickly, so I was very much alone at first . . . for quite awhile.

And then Hannah began to date and eventually married a really great guy.

Knowing where and what you're doing has so many advantages. On the other hand, I just muddle through, always wondering what next, wondering why God doesn't make it clear. I have a burden for ministry but, it seems, none of the "stuff" it takes to be involved in ministry. As I look at Hannah, I see the makings of a "somebody" God can use. I don't see the makings of anything in me.
Peninnah

The name of the person who seemingly caused these feelings of inadequacy isn't really Hannah. Neither, of course, is the writer's name Peninnah. But there was a Peninnah in biblical times, a woman seldom mentioned in all the sermons about Hannah, who may have felt very much like the writer of this painful letter I actually received.

Hannah's husband was Elkanah. And Peninnah was Elkanah's other wife.

The Bible clearly states in 1 Samuel 1:5 that Elkanah loved Hannah. Because Hannah's name is mentioned before Peninnah's (1 Sam. 1:2), it would seem to indicate that Hannah was Elkanah's first wife. Then why did Elkanah, a priest of the tribe of Levi,[2] take a second wife?

The answer seems quite obvious. Hannah was barren.

Barrenness—the recurring nightmare of beloved, beautiful women like Sarai, Rebekah, and Rachel! And as we discovered with Sarai in chapter 2, the inability to bear children involved much more than emotional frustration and yearning. A woman who could not bear children was considered useless, a nobody in the Hebrew community. Her life had no significance.

Hannah may have participated in finding a second wife who could give her husband an heir. (Can you imagine "wife-shopping" with your husband?) They may have decided together on Peninnah, whose name means "coral." Probably Peninnah was strong and sturdy, perhaps beautiful as coral, a young woman who would bear Elkanah children fitting to his honorable heritage. Whatever appeared to be her original qualifications, her personality became as sharp and cutting as the coral for which she was named.

She became Hannah's adversary (1 Sam. 1:6).

Most sermons I have heard on this subject develop our sympathy for Hannah. Certainly she was the righteous one in this situation. But let's spend a little time thinking about Peninnah's possible reactions to the triangular marriage.

Hannah's first, and I am second,
*   and it will always be so . . .*
I have borne Elkanah children,
*   but his love I'll never know.*
As they whisper in the darkness,
*   I draw close to my young sons.*

She is Rachel; I am Leah—
    Elkanah loves the childless one.

Oh, I hate her! How I hate her!
    Every time I see her tears
It reminds me that the future,
    all those long and lonely years,
Will be spent beside this woman
    who has all I'm longing for . . .
She is loved so very dearly,
    yet she reaches out for more.
If I cannot win Elkanah
    by the children I have borne,
Then, I swear, I'll make her pay.
    Hannah—rose beside the thorn!
And my thorns will prick her cruelly
    and I'll taunt her day by day,
Reminding her that she is barren,
    that her curse is here to stay.[3]

And that's exactly what lonely, loveless, frustrated Peninnah did. She punished Hannah for being the object of their husband's love.

The holidays, the sacrificial feasts, were the worst times of all. The beginning chapter of 1 Samuel relates a vignette during the time of the Feast of the Passover, when the entire family—Elkanah, childless Hannah, and Peninnah with "all her sons and daughters"—traveled to the tabernacle at Shiloh to make the yearly sacrifice.

This distance from Ramah to Shiloh was fifteen miles. We think of that as a short journey indeed. But not for this unhappy family! It would have taken at least two days by foot or donkey. Peninnah had no Pampers to pack for her little ones, no bottles for her babies. It must have been a very difficult trip for her.

And if Hannah offered her help, her "adversary" may have screamed: "What do you know about taking care of children? If the great Jehovah had wanted you to enjoy children, he would have given you your own! Just stay away from mine—and you can cry all you want to! It seems tears are all you can bring forth!"

When the day came that Elkanah sacrificed, he would give to Peninnah his wife, and all her sons and daughters, portions [of the sacrificial meat];
    But to Hannah he gave a double portion; for he loved Hannah. . . . [This embarrassed and grieved Hannah] and her rival provoked her greatly, to vex her, because the Lord had left her childless. (1 Sam. 1:4-6)

Every year at Christmas I take great care to insure that each of our three sons gets "equal coverage" in terms of gifts. In spite of all my efforts, however, when the time finally comes to take turns opening gifts, we never seem to come out even. Someone usually points out, half-jokingly, half-seriously, that "he got more than I did."

So it's easy to imagine how Peninnah must have felt when Hannah so obviously received preferential treatment. Especially when Peninnah heard Elkanah's gentle whispers to the miserably depressed Hannah: "Hannah, why do you cry? And why do you not eat? And why are you grieving? Am I not more to you than ten sons?" (1 Sam. 1:8).

Usually women are either "cry-ers" or "yell-ers." The more a yell-er yells, the more a cry-er cries. And the more the yell-er continues to yell, the more a cry-er continues to cry. What a vicious cycle!

Do you see that each woman in this tragic story was allowing the "other woman" to make her feel terribly inadequate? Isn't it a rerun of Sarai and Hagar or Rachel and Leah?

Hagar, Leah, and Peninnah lacked the security of being loved. Sarai, Rachel, and Hannah lacked the significance of pouring their love into young lives.

No matter how much we have (or others think we

have), no matter how great we look (or others think we look), no matter how intensely we are loved (or others think we are loved), as Pascal says, there is a God-shaped vacuum within each of us that only He can fill!

Until we absorb that fact, we will always have problems with inadequacy, insignificance, and insecurity. Not only in our heads, but also in our hearts.

Years ago Marilyn Monroe, the all-time American sex symbol, committed suicide. Why? That God-shaped vacuum was never filled in her life. Today many are committing different kinds of suicide—mental, moral, and spiritual suicide. Mental suicide can result from succumbing to wrong philosophy as well as to mind-altering drugs. Moral suicide is a final surrender to sensuality. Opening up oneself to the occult can lead to spiritual suicide.

Our God-shaped vacuum cannot be filled with money, sex, or power. Or, on a permanent basis, even with faithful human love like Elkanah's.

The following statements, quoted in chapter 2, are so important that I am repeating them:

Significance depends upon understanding who I am in Christ. I will come to feel significant as I have an eternal impact on people around me by ministering to them. If I fail in business, if my wife leaves me . . . I can still enjoy the thrilling significance of belonging to the Ruler of the universe, who has a job for me to do. He has equipped me for the job. As I mature by developing Christ-like traits, I will enter more and more fully into the significance of belonging to and serving the Lord.

My need for security demands that I be unconditionally loved, accepted and cared for, now and forever. God has seen me at my worst and still loved me to the point of giving His life for me. [4]

Hannah and Peninnah were both operating out of deficits in their lives. That fact they had in common—as well as living in the same house and being married to the same man.

When Hannah realized that only God could fill the need in her life and began to trust Him to do so, her life story began an upward spiral. There is no evidence that this happened in Peninnah's life.

What made the difference in their lives? What can make the difference in *our* inadequacies and frustrations?

Hannah knew where to turn to fill the vacuum.

The going wasn't easy. She had listened to her adversary's taunts for years. When she fled to the tabernacle to pour out her heart to God, she had to face a priest's accusation of drunkenness. (Perhaps Eli, the priest, was taking out his own frustrations on Hannah; his two sons had ruined their reputations by consorting with immoral women who hung around the tabernacle.) But Hannah looked past the people . . . to the Lord.

And [Hannah] was in distress of soul praying to the Lord, and weeping bitterly.

She vowed, saying, O Lord of hosts, if You will indeed look on the affliction of Your handmaid, and [earnestly] remember and not forget Your handmaid, but will give me a son, I will give him to the Lord all his life; no razor shall touch his head. (1 Sam. 1:10-11)

The solution to Hannah's problem could be found only in one Person. Hannah called Him the Lord of hosts—Jehovah-sabaoth.

"LORD SABAOTH IS HIS NAME"

The literal meaning of the word *sabaoth* is "to mass together" or "to assemble," and Jehovah-sabaoth is translated as "the Lord of hosts." This name of God, which many of us associate with old hymns of the church, depicts God as the Lord of the armies of Heaven. He is the captain of a myriad of angelic beings who are eternally loyal to Him and His every command. It is the same army that Jesus Christ, as commander-in-chief, will lead against Satan at the end of this age.

I saw heaven opened, and behold, a white horse [appeared]! The One Who was riding it is called Faithful . . . and True, and He passes judgment and wages war in righteousness. . . . And the troops of heaven, clothed in fine linen, dazzling and clean, followed Him on white horses.

From His mouth goes forth a sharp sword with which He can smite . . . the nations, and He will shepherd and control them with a staff . . . of iron. . . .

And on His garment (robe) and on His thigh He has a name (title) inscribed, KING OF KINGS AND LORD OF LORDS. *(Rev. 19:11, 14-16)*

This particular name of Jehovah was used only at times when Israel faced a crisis hour in history, and the days in which Hannah lived certainly fit that description. Although judges like Deborah and Gideon had tried to point the nation back to God, Israel had absorbed her Canaanite neighbors' heathen ways. Samson was physically strong, but morally he was one of the weakest judges. His sporadic leadership and dramatic downfall left Israel in a state of disillusionment and discouragement. With Samson's power no longer acting as a deterrent, the invading Philistines had begun a rule of terror.

The first use of the name Jehovah-sabaoth was in the first chapter of 1 Samuel, in the prayer of Hannah. Hannah was not praying for a son to satisfy her own needs, to please her husband, or to silence Peninnah's cutting barbs. She was not asking for just any child. She was asking for a man-child so that she could give him back to God to be used in His service, however He chose.

Men who were wholly the Lord's were sorely needed by Israel. Eli's sons offered no spiritual leadership to the nation. It was obvious that they were not able or willing to do this.

Herein lies the significance of Hannah's use of the name Jehovah-sabaoth in her prayer in 1 Samuel 1:11. The Lord of hosts could not rescue Israel from the invading Philistines until it had repented and turned back to God. Someone had to bridge the gap between the disobedient sons of Abraham and their yearning Creator, someone with a gracious spirit and an impassioned heart for the glory of God and the people of God.

Did you notice the repeated use of the word *handmaid* in Hannah's prayer? Even after her life's bitter humiliation of barrenness, even after her adversary's cutting taunts, even after the cruel reprimand from Eli, Hannah's spirit was gracious. Her request was unselfish.

And her request was granted by Jehovah-sabaoth. Hannah's son, Samuel, inherited her graciousness of spirit. One of the most important personalities in the Old Testament, he was greatly loved by the people he led. And he certainly possessed his mother's passion of heart. Bridging the period between the judges of Israel and the kings of Israel, he turned the children of Israel back to God.

Hannah's life seemed hopelessly barren. Her quiet, melancholy temperament didn't stand a chance against Peninnah's outspoken, aggressive personality. The contest seemed uneven, the outcome certain.

But God used Hannah's quiet and gentle spirit to leave an indelible impression on the sensitive little boy who was to become God's man for the hour. When Hannah visited Samuel each year, her faithful diligence provided him with a handmade coat, just as her faithful prayers no doubt covered him warmly throughout the year.

And as Hannah mothered the other children God gave her—three sons and two daughters, according to 1 Samuel 2:21—her feelings of insignificance changed to a heart knowledge of acceptability. No longer did Hannah need to retreat from the feast table to weep in the tabernacle. It was no longer necessary for Elkanah to reassure her of his love. The vacuum had been filled!

The knowledge that God had accepted His handmaiden's prayer—and His handmaiden—freed Hannah from herself. It freed her from her true adversary—her humiliation, her inadequacy—to use and develop the gifts God had given her.

God's unconditional acceptance is not based on our development of character. But that wonderful, life-giving acceptance, when realized internally, will spur us on to greater growth and faithfulness.

As I mature by developing Christ-like traits, I will enter more and more fully into the significance of belonging to and serving the Lord. [5]

Peninnah could have experienced a sense of significance also. Tragically, she probably never did.

Do your battles seem uneven? Does the outcome appear to be certain defeat? Have you faced ridicule and humiliation for so long that a breakdown or a breakaway seems a welcome alternative?

"O Lord of hosts, if You will indeed look on the affliction of Your handmaid. . . ."

If you have a Hannah-heart, a heart that knows Hannah's God, the Lord of hosts, the adversaries don't stand a chance.

WHAT IS THE MEANING OF HIS NAME?

Meditations of a Handmaiden. 1. On a scale of 1 (very poorly) to 10 (excellent), how do you feel about your roots (present family and heritage); your relationships (friends, neighbors, coworkers); your responsibilities?

2. For the most part, are your responsibilities:
   monotonous   frustrating   fulfilling   overwhelming

3. Complete this sentence: I feel loved and secure . . .

. . . hardly ever.

. . . when I am with certain people.

. . . most of the time.

. . . regardless of circumstances (because of who I am in Christ!).

4. Complete this sentence: My life seems to have purpose and I feel significant . . .

. . .hardly ever.

. . . when I am doing certain things (such as _____).

. . . regardless of circumstances (because of who I am in Christ and the gifts He has given me!).

5. It is easy to be His handmaiden in this area:_____.
It is hard to be His handmaiden in this area:_____.

6. The best handmaiden I know is _____
because she has the following qualities: _____
_____.

7. I can learn from her in the following way:_____.

8. The name Jehovah-sabaoth was used only at crisis times in history, when God's people needed to humble themselves, pray and seek His face, and turn from their wicked ways (2 Chron. 7:14). In what national or personal crisis do you need an understanding of that name?

9. I served as God's handmaiden this week by _____.

10. Today I will show my desire to be His handmaiden by _____.

Handmaiden Homework. Think about the compound truth of accountability and acceptability. In your life, which side of the coin needs more emphasis? If *acceptability* was your answer, read on!

What does the phrase "accepted in the beloved" (Eph. 1:6, KJV) mean to you? Tape these words on your mirror for a week and measure their effects. Perhaps you will want to leave them there!

As we respond to God's acceptance of us, we are freed to use creatively the gifts God has given each one of us. Begin a list of the abilities, talents, or gifts you feel stirring within you. You may think you don't have even one gift, but think about compliments people have given you; perhaps God was telling you something through them. Include things like the ability to praise or encourage your family members in special ways, such as through making a treat or item of clothing.

Think again about times people have said: "You're so good at . . ." or "I appreciate your . . ." What gifts might God be trying to encourage in you? Which are most important in the long run? In His service?

In the movie *Chariots of Fire,* future missionary Eric Liddell said: "When I run I feel God's pleasure. . . ."

When do *you* feel God's pleasure? There lies yet another clue to your gifts.[6]

7

Will I Ever Be Able to Put the Past Behind Me?

JEHOVAH-NISSI:
God is my banner
JEHOVAH-SHALOM:
God is my peace

On a Thursday evening in May I was at home alone, enjoying my favorite TV show—the only one, in fact, that I make time for consistently. Usually *The Bill Cosby Show* makes me laugh. But that evening it featured a college commencement ceremony at the Huxtables' alma mater. Unexpectedly, I found myself in tears.

I had just remembered that neither of my parents, although both were living and within an hour's drive at the time, had attended my college graduation ceremonies. My disappointment expressed itself twenty years after the fact!

After I stopped crying, I tried to analyze my reactions. Our oldest son was about to graduate from high school and head for college in Georgia. My memories of past disappointments had produced a present fear—the fear of losing the closeness we enjoy as a family.

Undoubtedly memory plays a powerful role in influencing our thoughts, attitudes, and ensuing actions.

In his book *Healing of Memories,* Dr. David Seamands points out that the verb "to remember" or "to call to mind a remembrance" is mentioned more than 250 times in Scripture. About seventy-five of these references are to God and His memory, many of them being requests that God remember something, such as His covenants, His promises, or His people. Some are requests for Him *not* to remember something—our sins and our failures, for example.

Dr. Seamands comments further:

In Scripture, memory is considered one of the most important aspects of both God's mind and ours. It is central to God's nature as well as to forgiveness, salvation, and righteous living. God's ability to remember or not remember is a part of the divine mind or knowledge which filled the Biblical writers with awe. Since we have been created in the divine image, we too have this ability. [1]

And this very ability to remember the past often causes problems in the present.

In some areas we, like God, can choose whether to remember or not remember. By an act of the will, I can decide whether or not to hold a grudge against someone who has offended me. I may choose to postpone punishment for a teenager's disobedience until his father comes home and a disciplinary decision can be made.

At other times, however, the ability to remember or not remember is not so easily regulated. Some memories of the past persist in attacking our conscious or unconscious minds—as in dreams—and greatly influence our present attitudes and actions.

Just as the rings of a tree reveal its developmental history, so our memories, lying underneath the veneer of our "bark," reveal the past realities of our lives. Unlike the rings of a tree, however, these remnants of the past come to life again, often at the most unexpected moments.

The recorded rings of my past—happy ones and sad

ones—are inextricably bound together. At times the negative memories have seemed almost overwhelming in their unexpected impact. Realizing this, I wonder how some children survive their pasts—and then go on to cope with adulthood.

Take Becky for example.

WHAT DO YOUR RINGS REVEAL?

The first time I heard Becky sing, something impressed me. This young woman had more than just a beautiful voice. I sensed a depth in her message, like the unmistakable fragrance emanating from a flower that has been crushed and broken. She had been hurt, but also healed.

My husband whispered to me, "You should talk to her." I nodded. "I know."

We did talk after the church service, and Becky told me a little bit about her life. I asked her to write and tell me more.

Here is the story of her life in Becky's own words, told with her permission.

I was born August 3, 1960. My mother and father were in the midst of a divorce. My father didn't want children and tried to choke my mother when she told him that she was pregnant. She then went to live with her parents, and the divorce was final after I was born.

My father tried to prove that I was not his so that he wouldn't have to pay child support, but the tests all came out proving that I was definitely his. Ironically, I have always looked exactly like him. I don't look at all like my mother.

After a couple of years my mother remarried. She had two sons by her second husband, who had lied about his age and was three years younger than she. He also had an alcohol problem and, when my mother met him, he was running away from the law. He had gotten a fifteen-year-old girl pregnant, and her father was trying to get him to marry her, go to jail, or join the military. He married my mother (she was pregnant) and thus began several horrible years of abuse, separations, welfare, etc. I can vividly remember my mother beaten and lying out in the driveway of our country house when I came home from kindergarten one afternoon.

My mother was developing phobias at the time, which she still has. Among them are the fears of riding in a car and riding in an elevator. I picked up several of her fears.

After some stormy years, my mother divorced [her second husband] and we spent our lives moving in and out of her parents' home or living in cheap apartments in the area. Very little in my life at this time had any stability except for going to church. I had accepted the Lord at the age of five and had always gone to church. Mainly, because it was the right thing to do and I could always find acceptance among the people.

My mother married again when I was eleven. This guy was fifty. She was thirty-one. This marriage uprooted us and took us to another town just long enough to find out that they were not compatible. At this time, I had a lot of problems sleeping. His house seemed to make me nervous. It was a huge farmhouse and I slept upstairs all by myself.

What had begun as just a nervous problem turned into a full-blown phobia. As soon as each day started turning into dusk, I became nervous. The first few months that we lived [in the farmhouse], I couldn't sleep very well. We moved back to our hometown at the end of the summer and tried to start our lives over again.

By this time, I was in the eighth grade. My problems with anorexia started at this time. What began as just a diet turned into several years of lying and near-starvation. Eventually my urinary tract broke down and I was hospitalized.

Although the *power* of God was not visible in Becky's life at this time, the *plan* of God was at work. (I am reminded of a German word I remember from Old Testament Survey in my freshman year of college. *Heiligeschichte,* as Dr. Shrag regularly reminded us, was the story of God's redemptive work through *all* of history.)

Becky had attended church because she felt secure there. She had memorized Scripture because it was "the thing to do." She had even walked an aisle to publicly accept Jesus Christ as Savior. But during her mother's second divorce and remarriage, Becky and her mother stopped attending church.

Later, however, while "in the depths of anorexia," as Becky describes it, she started back to church again. Somehow she had to get her life back together. But she felt full of anger and jealousy toward others whose lives were different from hers.

Today Becky looks back and says: "The reality of grace had not hit me because I had not recognized the presence of sin in my own life. It was too easy to blame my mother or others. I could not experience the joy of freedom from sin until I saw the nature of my anger, my jealousy, my deceitfulness."

At the age of twenty-one, while she was living in Germany with her soldier-husband, Becky saw herself as a sinner for the first time. Christianity was not a set of rules; it was a vital relationship with a living Person!

And now that Person could continue His plan for Becky's life. He could begin the healing of her past so that her miseries could be turned into ministries. Here's how Becky described the changes to me in her letter.

I had almost forgotten all about my struggle [with anorexia]. I probably had repressed it and stuffed it down because of the pain. This past weekend the Lord brought up this time in my life. He needed to deal with it. I was asked by The Alliance Witness *if I would review a book. This book was all about one woman's struggle with this oppression [of anorexia] and how she had almost died.*

I had kept the memories of this part of my life submerged in my subconscious. While reading this book, the Lord showed me what bondage I am now free of. One of the biggest fetters was all of the fear, deceit, and lying that goes along with that disease. You feel that everyone is your enemy and that you have to hide the fact that you are not eating, even if you must lie.

This horrible habit [of lying] had stayed with me even after my body had regained its normal weight and I was eating correctly. The mind games that you play with yourself and others are nothing but out-and-out deceit. I really praise God that He revealed this to me. He showed me a few years ago that I had a problem with lying, but just last weekend I realized that it was because of the deceitfulness of anorexia, not just because of my mother's mental problems. I had always blamed my mother for this.

I am truly a different person now than I was then. The Lord has taken specific memories and healed them, and also delivered me from bondages of fear. . . . The Lord never brings up all of your past at once, but piece by piece as you are able to handle it.

I recommended two books by Dr. David Seamands to Becky: *Healing of Memories* and *Putting Away Childish Things*. I made sure we discussed the use and abuse of the procedure known as the "healing of memories." The following is Dr. Seamands' own warning:

Healing of memories is a form of Christian counseling and prayer which focuses the healing power of the Spirit on certain types of emotional/spiritual problems. It is one and only one of such ministries, and should never be made the one and only form, for such overemphasis leads to exaggeration and misuse. It is very important that Christian workers possess both sufficient knowledge and Spirit-sensitized discernment to know when it is the right tool of the Spirit for healing.[2]

Becky told of her own experience with the healing of memories in another letter:

I found out about inner healing three years ago at a women's conference in Germany. I was playing the piano at this retreat and just happened to attend a workshop where a lady gave her testimony about how the Lord had healed her self-image. I went to my room and prayed about why I didn't want children. I had been married for about three and one-half years at the time. Not only did I not want children, but the thought of being pregnant made me want to kill myself. I didn't want to harm the child, but myself.

During a time of prayer, the Lord revealed the root of the problem—my rejection by my father. He then gave me a thought picture in my mind of me being born and His being there and picking me up in His arms as I came out from my mother. It was a time of healing and the start of a work that has been going on in my life ever since.

Recently I attended a Deeper Life Renewal weekend which the Christian & Missionary Alliance is putting on all over the nation to help people understand sanctification. This series of meetings helped me to understand a lot more about emotional healing.

In my own case, I did not have a "counselor" other than the Holy Spirit. It was in my quiet time alone with the Lord that the healing took place and still takes place. I came to the realization that it is the Lord using whatever means He chooses to use that does the healing; if He chooses to use our imagination and mind to help us feel His presence, then it can't be wrong. But the more important and essential element is the Lord and our coming to Him to be made new, not the technique. Emotional healing comes as we get closer to the Lord and become more like Him. No method or technique does the healing; He does as He renews our minds.

So the method should not get the emphasis, but coming closer to the Lord and becoming more like Him should be what we preach and teach. Our job is to point people to Him and to concentrate on learning His Word and coming into His presence. His job is the healing and renewing of our minds, bodies, and spirits.

I used to feel that we needed to heal people emotionally so that they could become closer to God, but now I feel that this healing is a benefit that comes from becoming more like Him. It is actually a part of our sanctification.

WHEN FEAR ATTACKS: FIGHT OR FLIGHT?

Perhaps as you read Becky's words, you yearned wholeheartedly to be rid of leftovers from the past. But that goal seems unreachable. It might be good to review the lives of some Bible characters who also struggled with inhibitions due to past experiences. Rereading Exodus 3 and 4 gives new insights.

Moses has had to flee his native land because of his murder of a fellow Egyptian. During this desert time in his life he becomes a shepherd, taking his flocks to the back side of the wilderness, the "mountain of God"—Mt. Horeb or Sinai. It is here that God speaks to Moses from a burning bush and calls Moses to lead his people out of Egypt.

By this time, however, Moses has not only spent forty years in the palace of Pharaoh, but also forty years in the desert-wilderness. He has come to doubt every natural ability that had been developed and educated in the courts of Pharaoh. He is not even sure how much he understands about the God of his fathers, this God who allowed Him to be displaced from his people shortly after birth and then seemingly deserted him in the desert.

Moses' wavering response to God's call is understand-able. First he asks the question most of us would ask: "Who am I?"

Next he asks: "Who are You?"

The first question sounds humble. The second question sounds logical; after all, if I'm expected to totally change my life-style, I need to know whose directions I'm following.

God's answer to Moses' first question is simple: "I will be with you."

His answer to the second question is enigmatic: "I AM

WHO I AM and WHAT I AM, and I WILL BE WHAT I WILL BE"
(Exod. 3:14).

As discussed earlier, another way of interpreting the
meaning of God's name is central to understanding his
nature: "I am becoming whatever you need."

*In Exodus 3:14 we find the name that God asked the man Moses
to reveal to Israel! God's name, Yahweh, comes from the Hebrew
verb,* hayah, *which means "to be"! God is not being facetious
here, but is saying, "I will be whatever you need me to be to get
the job done!" I am strength, I am food, I am safety, I am
healing, I am deliverer, I am the ticket to your troubles and your
triumphs! This is a gigantic theological statement on the theology
of our God! He is, was, and ever shall be the great I AM! He is the
Divine panacea, the cure-all for the ills, spills, and hills of
humanity![3]*

Moses was hearing, but not understanding. Exodus 4
deals with his excuses. He protested that nobody would
believe this great God had sent him. And God answered
again by taking the rod—the symbol of Moses' everyday,
mundane employment, the symbol of his identity as a
shepherd—and turning it into a serpent.

As Moses well knew, the serpent was the symbol of royal
and divine power worn on the crown of the Pharaohs.

In this symbolism was the truth that God had amply
prepared Moses for his calling. First by forty years of
leadership training in the court of Pharaoh. Then by forty
lonely desert years to chisel his "palace-spoiled" character.

No experience is ever wasted in the providence of God!

But when the rod became a serpent, Moses fled from it.
He was in fear of God's message, afraid of God's claim on
his life. Possibly he feared going back to Egypt and facing
the consequences of murdering a man. Perhaps he feared
embarrassment in front of his old palace buddies.

Zipporah, his Midianite wife, might not understand his
call from God. "Your God spoke out of a flaming cactus?

Really, my husband, you have been out in the sun too long!"

Moses' reactions revealed a lot of things about the rings of his life. He gave God three reasons why he was not the man for the job:

1. My credibility: They won't believe that my message is from the Lord.
2. My lack of ability: I am not a good speaker.
3. My unavailability: I've put down roots here; please send someone else.

God had answers for all three:

1. I AM hath sent you; I will defend your credibility!
2. Who made your mouth? Who decided what ability you should have? Who's in control here—you or Me?
3. I am sending someone else—your brother, Aaron—but you must go with him. Take this rod in your hand, with which you *shall* work the signs (that prove I sent you). Now get going!

Evidently Moses learned his lesson. In Numbers 12:8 he is described by God as a trusted servant with whom He spoke face to face.

Once the matter of Moses' availability was settled, the question of his ability was taken care of by the Creator of all true credibility.

THE ROD OF GOD

Years later, when Joshua succeeded Moses, Moses' rod was recognized as the symbol of God's ultimate leadership. It had writhed into a serpent in Pharaoh's presence. It had been stretched out over the waters of Egypt as they turned to blood and later bred thousands (probably millions!) of loathsome frogs. It had divided the Red Sea in an awesomely miraculous deliverance.

The rod of God represented many faith-building memories.

And now God was grooming another man for leadership.

Exodus 17 tells the story of Joshua's first battle against Israel's archenemy, the Amalekites, who were descendants of Amalek, a grandson of Esau. These relatives of the Israelites had chosen to remember Esau's old grudge against his brother Jacob and were Israel's enemy.

Remember what Amalek did to you on the way, when you had come forth from Egypt; How he did not fear God, but when you were faint and weary he attacked you along the way and cut off all the stragglers in your rear. (Deut. 25:17-18)

Memories of Amalek's guerrilla tactics probably struck fear deep into the heart of the Israelites. Amalek had a way of sneaking up from behind, ambushing and surprise-attacking the Israelites at their weakest moments.

(Isn't that the way bad memories strike—an ambush, a surprise attack, just when you think the past is all behind · you?)

But God's directions to Joshua, through Moses, were very clear: "Don't run! *Fight!*" And both Moses and Joshua followed orders well.

Well, you say, I would expect Moses to have conquered fear by this point in his life. But what about young, inexperienced Joshua?

Joshua had seen God's power demonstrated through Moses time after time—and evidently he did not forget what he had witnessed, as so many of the Israelites did.

The most recent miracle had been the water that emerged from the rock at Mt. Horeb, located toward the southern point of the Sinai Peninsula, where almost a year later the law was given. The northern part of the Sinai Peninsula is desert; the southern part is a rugged mountainous area known for its mines of copper, iron, ochre, and precious stones. Hardly a place to find water! But Elohim had created water where there was none.

Faith-building memories had replaced any fear that remained in Joshua's mind.

And Moses said to Joshua, Choose us out men, and go out, fight with Amalek. Tomorrow I will stand on the top of the hill with the rod of God in my hand.

So Joshua did as Moses said and fought with Amalek; and Moses, Aaron, and Hur went up to the hilltop. (Exod. 17:9-10)

If the hill that Moses referred to here was again Mt. Sinai, the trio's ascent to the top would have taken much time and energy. *Halley's Bible Handbook* describes Sinai as "an isolated mass of rock, rising abruptly from the plain in awful grandeur."[4] On the northwest side is a plain, two miles long and one-half mile wide, where Israel could have encamped. When the three men reached the top, they would have been just barely visible to the people.

But Joshua knew that Moses held the rod of God, the banner of Jehovah-sabaoth, the Lord of hosts! (In those days a banner was not necessarily a flag; it could simply be a stick or pole with an object attached that would glisten in the sun.)

"When Moses held up his hand, Israel prevailed; and when he lowered his hand, Amalek prevailed" (Exod. 17:11). Human hands were not the source of power in this situation. Human hands had not released the thirst-quenching water a few days earlier. Human hands simply *held* the rod, the symbol of God's power.

But Moses' hands were heavy and grew weary. So [the other men] took a stone and put it under him, and he sat on it. Then Aaron and Hur held up his hands, one on one side and one on the other side; so his hands were steady until the going down of the sun.

And Joshua mowed down and disabled Amalek and his people with the sword.

And Moses built an altar and called the name of it, The Lord is my banner. (Exod. 17:12-13, 15)

Jehovah-nissi—the Lord my banner, the Power that enables me to move ahead.

Amalek—the symbol of that thing that inhibits my progress. It may be a present problem, or it may be an unwelcome memory.

In our own power, we are helpless. But when the rod of God, the banner of Jehovah, is held high, we are more than conquerors!

"ENEMIES LIKE LOCUSTS FOR MULTITUDE"

I always welcome letters from Barb. They are refreshingly candid, expressing real, honest-to-goodness feelings: loneliness, joy, anger, sensitivity to others' hurts. They discuss real doubts and depression that sometimes result from past or present pain. And they reflect real faith.

Barb is a missionary.

Barb is also single and often very much alone. Not only that—her family members back home in the States do not understand why she is in another country.

Barb explained her relationship with her family in one of her letters:

You asked about my family . . .

I fear that I often forget that I do indeed have a family. How is it that something that God created to be beautiful also at times produces such guilt and so many marks in one's life?

I have a very average family. At the moment I am the only believer. They are not opposed to what I'm doing, they just don't understand why I am so far away.

My mother suffers the most. She thinks that if I were near she would have someone to help her solve her problems. She forgets that we have never been friends. And I still think of her as Mom, not as some person that I might enjoy knowing.

It is extremely difficult for me to maintain contact with them. I have never been a good letter writer, mostly because I never knew what to say to them. While my mother demands letters from me, she is worse than I about writing. But lately I have felt the need to be more open with them about my ministry. So I am trying to write more frequently, short letters but more frequent.

It is hard for me to handle guilt feelings when my mom starts telling me how much she needs me. I have two married brothers, one of whom lives on the farm with my folks. But I'm the only daughter. We never developed any kind of close relationship for a number of reasons, and I suppose the guilt comes from my seeming inability to respond in kind to my mother's need (or demand) for attention.

Plus, and this sounds cruel but perhaps you will understand, I have a hard time "feeling" any kind of love for my parents. I love them in the sense that they are my parents and they have given me much. I know that in any emergency, etc., I would want to be with them. And I know that if I have certain needs they are always there. It is all rather complicated.

My sympathy goes out to all parents. Mine tried to the best of their ability to raise three children—well-mannered, educated, and self-reliant. They didn't know how to teach us to show affection or to accept and love others with differing opinions and ideas. We turned out to be well-mannered, somewhat educated, and too self-reliant. All three of us have difficulty expressing love and affection. All three of us tend to be intolerant of differing ideas, and all three of us tend to think we aren't worth much.

My brothers have a hard time accepting the fact that my folks did the best they could with what they had. My healing process began the day I gave myself to the Lord. It's still going on. I can understand and accept what my folks did. I can understand my brothers' point of view. But I feel impotent in terms of changing anything. Mostly I feel a failure in terms of my own attitudes as a Christian. So, with God helping, I am seeking ways to bring some changes to my way of communicating with my folks.

Well, I didn't mean to go on so much about that. As you can perhaps perceive, one of my biggest burdens is this whole area. Perhaps I make too much of it. I am just beginning to discover

*the tremendous influence my mother has had in my life. Some
good, but mostly the kind that inhibits. She doesn't know it and
certainly it's not what she intended. Unfortunately, good
intentions often don't make it into actions that are positive.*

*The lessons I've learned and am learning are invaluable as I
seek to deepen my relationship with God and minister to others.
Compassion grows out of experiences appreciated and applied to
greater understanding. I may not have many answers, but I
think I have a good measure of compassion for parents and for
the products they so unwittingly produce.*

Barb's letter reminded me of a biblical character who
was asked by God to do something his family did not
understand. The man was Gideon, a member of a poor
family in the insignificant tribe of Manasseh. God chose
him to lead Israel against their enemies, the Midianites.

First, however, he had to destroy the family altar!

Let's backtrack a little to understand. After the time of
Moses and Joshua, the Israelites had rejected Jehovah and
turned to the worship of Baal. God sent the Midianites to
punish them.

*And they would encamp against them and destroy the crops . . .
and leave no nourishment for Israel, and no ox or sheep or
donkey.*

For they came . . . like locusts for multitude. . . . *and the
Israelites cried to the Lord. (Judg. 6:4-6, emphasis mine)*

God heard their cry. He appeared personally to Gideon
and told him that he was the man for the hour.

When his visitor came, Gideon was beating wheat,
hiding his activity in a winepress so that the Midianites
would not see him and take his meager supply of food.

Gideon's reply in Judges 6:15 sounds just like Moses'
"Who-am-I" question: "Who, *me*? How can I deliver
Israel? I'm the least important person in my family, and my

family is the poorest in Manasseh" (paraphrase mine).

Gideon's reply revealed his "rings"—and his low opinion of himself.

God's answer was unchanging, the same one He had given to Moses: "Surely I will be with you."

Gideon's second response was an echo of Moses' "Who-are-you" question: "Show me a sign that it's You, Lord."

Graciously, God gave Gideon a sign. Fire came down from heaven and consumed Gideon's offering. When the Angel of the Lord disappeared from sight, Gideon realized that he had actually spoken with God Himself, and he was afraid for his life.

Alas, O Lord God! For now I have seen the Angel of the Lord face to face!

The Lord said to him, Peace be to you; do not fear, you shall not die.

Then Gideon built an altar there to the Lord, and called it, The Lord is peace. (Judg. 6:22-24)

Jehovah-shalom—the Lord is peace!

Gideon realized that not only *is* the Lord peace, but that He will *bring* peace to His people when they obey His voice. That is the contingency of Jehovah-shalom.

God instructed Gideon to tear down his father's altar to Baal (the Phoenician sun-god), cut down the Asherah (a sacred pole, cone of stone, or tree trunk that represented the goddess Astoreth and was often erotic in nature), and build an altar to the Lord God "on top of this stronghold" (Judg. 6:26). Then Gideon was to offer a burnt sacrifice, using the very wood of the Asherah!

Gideon now believed God had called him, but he was still inhibited by his background. His fear of his father's household and of the men of the city made him decide to do God's bidding—but at night, when no one would see him. Then Gideon hid, perhaps in the winepress again, while the men of the city searched for the destroyer of their sacred sin-center.

Poor Gideon! The enemy Midianites had seemed "like locusts for multitude." That was bad enough. Now even his friends, down to the members of his father's household, had become his enemies—all because he was obedient to God.

Was this the result of following Jehovah-shalom, the God of peace?

Then the men of the city commanded Joash [Gideon's father], Bring out your son, that he may die. . . .

But Joash said to all those who stood against him, Will you contend for Baal? Or will you save him? . . . If Baal is a god, let him contend for himself. . . . (Judg. 6:30-31)

Gideon was obedient to God, and God rewarded him. His father defended him. More important . . .

The Spirit of the Lord clothed Gideon with Himself and took possession of him; and he blew a trumpet, and [the clan of] Abiezer was gathered after him.

And he sent messengers throughout all Manasseh, and the Manassites were called to follow him; and he sent messengers to Asher, to Zebulun, and to Naphtali, and they came up to meet them. (Judg. 6:34-35)

When we are clothed with God Himself, possessed by Him, there is no room for leftovers from the past. We are at peace.

Read for yourself the rest of Gideon's thrilling story. He started out with 32,000 men. He lost 22,000 who were "fearful and trembling" (Judg. 7:3). Even then God kept reducing the number—finally down to 300—so that it would be very clear exactly whose power was at work!

Gideon's name means *one who cuts down.* Our inhibiting

memories may be "like locusts for multitude," but the banner of Jehovah-nissi goes before us reminding us of one thing: "Greater is He that is in you than he that is in the world" (1 John 4:4, KJV).

And it is as we obey His directions to destroy the traps of the enemy that He becomes Jehovah-shalom, our peace.

WHAT IS THE MEANING OF HIS NAME?

1. Do you find it difficult to believe that God "chooses not to remember" certain things from your past that you have asked Him to forgive?

2. What warning does Dr. David Seamands give concerning counseling centered around the healing of memories? What caution does Becky Puchy add?

3. What were some of Moses' fears? How does doubt about one's credibility and/or lack of ability affect one's availability to God?

4. How are Amalek's guerrilla tactics symbolic of inhibiting or fear-inspiring memories?

5. Find Mt. Sinai on a map of the Exodus. Why was finding water at Mt. Sinai so miraculous? Use a Bible concordance to help you discover and discuss other Old Testament stories in which Mt. Sinai, also known as Mt. Horeb, played a part. How does God use certain geographical locations in our lives? Do you have a personal Mt. Sinai?

6. Moses' shepherd rod was used by God as a banner to lead His people to victory. Why was it necessary for Moses' hands to be upraised while Joshua fought his first battle? What did this imply about the true source of leadership?

7. The Midianites were enemies of Israel who seemed like "locusts for multitude." Imagine a community's reaction to an invasion of locusts. Why did God allow the Midianite

invasion? Have you ever experienced a spiritual or emotional "invasion"?

8. How did Gideon feel about his ability? His credibility? His availability? What was his fear?

9. Jehovah-shalom became Gideon's source of peace as he obeyed divine direction. In what area is God urging you to obey?

10. "The Spirit of the Lord clothed Gideon with Himself" (Judg. 6:34). Letting God's Spirit rule within us is the best possible preparation for battling the enemy. Since our enemies are not people but "persons without bodies" (Eph. 6:12, TLB), what kind of combat clothing is needed? (See Eph. 6:14-17.) Is a "camouflage" outfit included in the list? Why or why not?

8

*Why Doesn't God
Do Something?*

EL ELYON:
The Most High God
EL ROI:
The God who sees

I grew up with a lot of anger around me. That anger was
the source of hurt and confusion in my life and the lives of
others. Perhaps it was only natural, then, that I came to the
conclusion that anger is wrong. That anger is always sinful.

But I had to deal with my own anger. I didn't know how
to express it constructively. No one had taught me. My role
model, my mother, very seldom showed anger in any
situation; I realize now that she simply repressed it.

No one acknowledged my feelings of anger. And I didn't
want to hurt others. So for years I too repressed the anger
that came to a sudden boil within me. Or let it dissolve into
frustrated tears that temporarily cooled my ventilation
system but left a noxious residue. Or simply tried to get
away from the heat!

Sometimes, however, the anger continued to simmer,
turning into resentment and then bitterness. Eventually my
stifled emotions cooled, finally freezing into a sort of numb
depression.

This cycle occurred over and over again before I learned

that anger is *not* necessarily sinful, that Jesus Himself felt anger and expressed it. Different kinds of anger simply need to be handled in different ways. I began to see that Jesus' example encourages us to find constructive ways of dealing with this volatile emotion that is so capable of hurting—but also helping!—others. I realized that my own anger could be put to good use.

We discussed anger in our community Bible study. Barb, who is living with several teenagers, made this observation:

When I repress justifiable anger— "righteous indignation"—or do not express it in a constructive manner, in the way God urges me to, that same anger comes leaking out, bit by bit, in frustrations over little things like spilled milk at the breakfast table. And then it's not *righteous!*

How do we express anger constructively? Writing is one of the best ways I have found. Writing down the reasons for your anger has several advantages over expressing it verbally.

You can put your anger "on hold" for several days and then reread it, watching for the overemotional, illogical thinking that often accompanies anger. Many family arguments could be avoided if an explanatory note, giving reasons for certain feelings, were shared rather than shouted! Also, after time has passed, any "pity-party thinking" becomes obvious.

Justifiable anger can motivate constructive reactions such as letters to the editor. Who can measure the potential for persuasion through well-measured words? When Scripture is quoted, God has promised that His Word will not return void.

The following is a letter I felt compelled to write. Although it was published in our local newspaper, I never received any feedback from the public. Nonetheless, I had the inner peace of knowing I had done "a right thing."

Dear Editor,

On Sunday evening, July 27, I was alone at home and spent some time switching TV channels. Our family watches very little TV and I decided to see what we were missing.

In viewing five minutes of one program I watched three different couples in bed (or in a hurry to get there). The plot—if there was one—didn't hold my interest, so I moved to another channel where I quickly became involved in the story of a young mother trying to support her three children by working in a nonunion sweatshop. It was a welcome change to see acting that involved more than dressing and undressing, so I stayed with the story for some time.

I soon realized, however, that this scriptwriter had chosen to introduce the local rescue mission as the villain. According to the story, the director of the union rescue mission tricked the mother into signing adoption papers for her children rather than the medical release she thought she was signing. While the brave little mother was working and sweating away, the evil directress whisked away the children.

I have worked with rescue missions and know that they are actively involved in things like feeding the hungry families of alcoholics and rehabilitating the alcoholics themselves. Had my children watched this program, however, they certainly would not have received this impression. They would have been afraid to even visit a place like Bethesda Mission, York or Hagerstown Union Rescue Mission, or numerous other places of refuge.

As a parent, I am angry that it has become necessary for me to monitor TV viewing in order to prevent my children from drawing distorted conclusions. How long will the American public continue to tolerate untrue and unfair propaganda?

A concerned citizen

I realize now that I should have sent my letter to the advertisers who supported the program. As my Pennsylvania Dutch ancestors would have said, "We get too soon old—and too late smart!"

DO I PROVOKE ANGER IN OTHER PEOPLE?

Several years ago at a writer's conference, I listened to carefully expressed anger. It came from an unexpected source—someone I would have described as "a quiet little Amish girl."

Each writer had been given the opportunity to participate in a poetry coffeehouse. A slim young woman in dark dress and stockings, wearing the traditional Amish prayer covering, walked calmly to the microphone. She made her contribution without introduction in a clear, unflinching voice.

TOURISTS

How sad that they never look past our clothes.
If they did, they'd see Ben is the best carpenter there is.
Kind, compassionate, not just a broad-rimmed Amishman.
But they watch him plowing and all they know are the horses,
the suspenders, the beard.

It's too bad they never see beyond our clothes.
They see my white cap and wonder how I get it to stand so stiff
And why my skirt is so long and my stockings so black.
But they care not a whit for my spirit, my yearnings, my thoughts.

One would think we'd been stuffed and put in a museum
And had the feelings and intelligence of a wooden post
The way they gape and discuss among themselves, acting so smug,
"If only Cousin Bernie could see this!" snapping pictures, staring, staring.

What can you expect, though, from people who think milk comes from the store?
Who all look alike, the men with bald faces and knobby knees,
The women with short, dyed hair and long, painted fingernails,
Letting their children be rude; pointing at me, "Look, Mom! There's one!"

Brooklynites all, they talk through their noses, drive powder-blue Cadillacs,
And learn nothing from their trip to Lancaster, Pennsylvania,
Because they never look past our clothes.

—*Bonnie Hellum Brechbill*[1]

The controlled anger in the poem was justified. I remember well the feeling that all of us in that college cafeteria shared for a few moments as Bonnie's words impacted our conscious or unconscious prejudices. As I joined in the applause that followed the thoughtful silence, I wondered how often I too had evaluated people on the basis of surface signals.

Bonnie had found a constructive outlet for her anger.

Bonnie also had the fulfillment of meeting at least a handful of people who listened to and understood her feelings.

Many people share Bonnie's reactions to being treated like a museum piece. Many, however, never get the opportunity to communicate their feelings. Larry is an example.

By occupation, Larry is a computer programmer, but his brain is unable to successfully program his body into coordinated action. Larry suffered brain damage while enrolled in medical school; as a result, his speaking ability is impaired. He is able to communicate only by means of a portable communicator strapped to his body.

Because of Larry's problem in communicating and his muscular spasticity, many opportunities for friendship and fellowship degenerate into "staring, staring"—as if, to use Bonnie's words, Larry had "the feelings and intelligence of a wooden post." I have often wished that some of his not-so-intelligent observers could read the letters he punches into a computer! Here is one, reprinted with Larry's permission.

Dear _____ ,

A sudden realization has just come over me: I'm getting old. I will be thirty-three this October 12th, the same age when Jesus died. And what do I have to show for it all, huh? A pocket full of pills, a pretty nice stereo system (whenever I get the opportunity to use it, i.e., whenever I'm not glued to my TV or my VCR), a sophisticated line of communication devices (a TTV and a voice synthesizer, not to mention my two Canon Communicators).

But what do I really have to show for myself, for thirty-two years of God-given life, that is of any eternal value? Not much, I'm afraid to say, considering that nearly one-third of my life on this planet has been trapped in a malfunctioning body. And now, it never seems to end—the frustration and the trying to live a normal life. If anything, it just seems to get harder.

"Who will deliver me from this sinful, broken body?" Romans 7 and 8 is the correct answer, but why isn't there more evidence of the new man in my life? It seems that whenever I want to do good, evil is lurking right by the door ready to pounce on me.

I know that you, most probably, aren't faced with the dilemma I am—you who have progressed so much in your Christian life. But I am still being tempted by that old wily serpent, Satan. I hate to lay such a seemingly heavy burden on you, but I am looking for answers that don't disappear like a morning mist, answers that are concrete and solidly backed by the Word of God.

Thank you for listening to my problems and for your answers (i.e., assuming you have answers for me, which I don't blame you if you don't). The Lord bless you.

With love,
Larry

How much discouragement, hurt, and anger is caused simply by our unwillingness to break through communication barriers! Larry is a prime example. Although he is always eager to punch out messages on his communicator, few people take time to wait . . . and to affirm him by replying and waiting again. People who could choose to encourage others do just the opposite through their silence.

Joni Eareckson Tada says she is still caught off guard by cruel reminders that, in the minds of some people, a wheelchair marks her as mentally incompetent. This beloved author and speaker related recently how hurt and angry she had felt at being ignored by an airline assistant when she told him she knew her flight number. The airline personnel conversed above her head, implying she was incapable of understanding the question.

Empathizing with others is not an option for the Christian! We are directed to "share each other's troubles and problems, and so obey our Lord's command" (Gal. 6:2, TLB). We are also warned, "If anyone thinks he is too great to stoop to this, he is fooling himself. He is really a nobody" (Gal. 6:3, TLB).

WHAT IS THE FOCUS OF OUR ANGER?

When we feel that familiar fire flaring up inside, it is important to recognize the real focus of our anger. Is it a rerun of old, unhealed hurts? Or is it directed toward a problem person? Is it discontent concerning a situation that may need constructive action—perhaps initiated by me?

There is another possible focus of anger. I have realized that often my anger was not directed at outside sources of irritation, but at myself—or rather, at my too-high expectations of myself. And since my expectations of myself center around the gifts and responsibilities that God has given me, sometimes I find that my anger is really— though unconsciously—directed at God Himself.

The expectations of the perfectionist, as mentioned in chapter 3, can create a real predicament! Dr. David Seamands describes what happens after the perfectionist has lived with the "shouting shoulda's" for too long a time.

Something terrible is beginning to happen to the perfectionist. He may not realize it, but deep in his heart a kind of anger is developing. A resentment against the oughts, against the Christian faith, against other Christians, against himself, but saddest of all, against God.

Oh, not that it's really against the true God. That's the sadness of it; that's what breaks my heart. The perfectionist is not against the gracious, loving, self-giving God who has come to us, who in Jesus Christ went all the way to the Cross at such cost. No, his resentment is against a caricature of a god who is never satisfied. A god whom he can never please no matter how hard he tries, no matter what he gives up or holds on to. This cruel god always ups the ante a little, always demands a bit more and says, "Sorry, that wasn't quite good enough. . . ."

Too often the anger is not faced but denied. Because anger is considered a terrible sin, it is pushed down. And the whole mixture of bad theology, legalism, and salvation by performance becomes a frozen Niagara. This is when deep emotional problems set in. Mood changes are so great and terrible that such a person seems to be two different people at the same time.

Under the stress and the strain of trying to live with a self he can't like, a God he can't love, and other people he can't get along with, the strain can become too much. And one of two things can happen: Either there is a breakdown or a breakaway. *(Emphasis mine)[2]*

EXHAUSTED ELIJAH

In the story told in 1 Kings 18-19, the Old Testament prophet Elijah was close to either a breakdown or a breakaway. Elijah had been greatly angered by the actions of the wicked Queen Jezebel—a righteous anger, since she had cut off the prophets of the Lord. In the adrenalin-powered strength of that anger, Elijah had confronted the 450 prophets of Baal on Mt. Carmel. El Elyon, the Most High God, had demonstrated His power in a miraculous way, and the prophets of Baal were totally defeated.

Yet within hours of this amazing confrontation, Elijah was running for his life—from just one person, Queen Jezebel! He *broke away* from all ties with Israel, and he came very close to a *breakdown*.

Jezebel's name was used as a symbol of lewdness in Revelation 2:20. How did this wicked woman become Israel's queen?

Do you know the facts about this woman with the unsavory reputation? She lived in the ninth century B.C. and was the daughter of the Phoenician priest-king, Ethbaal, who murdered his own brother in cold blood. Ethbaal's lack of conscience seems to have been handed down to his daughter Jezebel.

As a king's daughter, Jezebel's wish had been her servants' command, and no ethical or moral implications were considered. Her marriage to Ahab was probably the result of an alliance between Ethbaal and Ahab's father, Omri. Her husband's obvious weakness of character contributed to her ruthlessness. (Although Ahab had a harem, no other wives are mentioned— only seventy sons!) A smaller kingdom than her father's and a childish monarch for a husband provided a fertile playground for this willful woman.

Jezebel's religion cost Ahab a lot of shekels! She supported (that means fed!) 450 prophets of Baal and 400 priests of Asherah. Her worship of these evil deities provided the religious basis for her activities, for she subscribed wholeheartedly to the philosophy of pleasure and self-centeredness. [3]

And Israel had blindly followed weak Ahab and willful Jezebel.

Through Elijah, God announced that Israel would be chastised by an extended drought. Then Elijah went into hiding. At the time of the Mt. Carmel confrontation, the countryside had felt neither rain nor dew for three years. Now God was ready to send a rainstorm!

Let's return to Mt. Carmel. Elijah's words were

memorable: "How long will you halt and limp between two opinions? If the Lord is God, follow Him! But if Baal, then follow him" (1 Kings 18:21).

Elijah then proposed a test. Two sacrifices would be chosen and laid on the altars of sacrifice. The people could observe which god—Baal or Jehovah—would send down fire from heaven to consume the sacrifice.

The 450 prophets of Baal called on their god from morning to noon. Then from noon until evening. They begged him to send down fire on their sacrifice. They even practiced self-mutilation, as was their custom, "but there was no voice, no answer, no one who paid attention" (1 Kings 18:29).

Finally, they gave up.

Painstakingly, alone, Elijah rebuilt the old altar of the Lord that had been broken down by Queen Jezebel. He enlarged the altar with twelve stones, representing the twelve tribes of Israel, "in the name [and self-revelation] of the Lord" (1 Kings 18:32). And he dug a trench around the altar.

After the sacrifice had been arranged on the altar, Elijah directed the people to fill four jars with water and to pour the water on the sacrifice. This was done three times, to insure the seeming impossibility of combustion and, again, to represent the twelve tribes.

And then Elijah called on his God. He addressed the Most High God—El Elyon.

O Lord, the God of Abraham, Isaac, and Israel, let it be known this day that You are God in Israel, and that I am Your servant, and that I have done all these things at Your word.

Hear me, O Lord, hear me, that this people may know that You, the Lord, are God, and have turned their hearts back [to You]. (1 Kings 18:36-37)

And fire came down from heaven! Fire that consumed not only the sacrifice but also the stone altar, the water-soaked kindling, and even the water in the trench Elijah had built!

Elijah had just survived what was probably the most grueling day of his life; the stress had been overwhelming. The prophets of Baal had not only been shown up, but also wiped out. The people seized the false prophets and, as Elijah directed, slew them by the Kishon Brook.

Finally, the hand of El Elyon released rain to a famine-stricken land.

"The hand of the Lord was on Elijah" (1 Kings 18:46). What a tremendous victory! God even gave Elijah strength to run ahead of Ahab's chariot from Mt. Carmel to Jezreel—a seventeen-mile run! Could Elijah ever again doubt the presence of El Elyon?

Yet the victory of the mountaintop is often followed by the inevitable descent into the valley.

Exhausted Elijah got a sudden shove down the emotional incline from a furiously angry queen who had just heard that Baal had lost the battle. Jezebel vowed to kill Elijah within twenty-four hours!

And the man who had just been humanly responsible for the one-day purge of evil from the land of Israel said: "I'm too tired to even think about what she's likely to do next. I'm certainly not going to waste my time being anxious about it. Lord, will You please do my thinking for me? I've obeyed Your orders and You've shown Your power so magnificently. So, Lord God of Israel, will you please take care of this crazy woman while I get some rest?"

Wrong! That's not what he said.

On the contrary . . .

Then he was afraid, and arose and went for his life, and came to Beersheba of Judah [over eighty miles, and out of Jezebel's realm] and left his servant there.

But he himself went a day's journey into the wilderness, and came and sat down under a lone broom or juniper tree, and

asked that he might die. He said, It is enough; now, O Lord,
take away my life. (1 Kings 19:3-4)

If Elijah was emotionally exhausted after the Mt. Carmel
ordeal, imagine his collapse after eighty miles of cross-
country confusion! He was ready to die.

Instead, he fell asleep.

The mighty El Elyon is also the gentle El Roi, a name
that originates in Genesis 16:13, the God who sees. The
God who knows when we have hit the pits. The God who
recognizes our need of nourishment, physical and spiritual.
The God who understands our intense yearning for
encouragement.

El Roi came to Elijah in the form of an angel, touched
him gently, and said, "Arise and eat."

When Elijah reluctantly opened his eyes, what did he
see? The fruit of the juniper tree? No, God had provided a
real meal—"a cake baked on the coals and a bottle of
water" (1 Kings 19:6). What concern El Roi showed for a
burnt-out prophet!

Elijah ate and drank, and exhaustion took over once
again.

El Roi was gentle, but there was a purpose for this
special care package. He touched Elijah again and gave the
aimless prophet a sense of direction:

The Angel of the Lord came the second time, and touched him,
and said, Arise and eat, for the journey is too great for you.

So he arose, and ate and drank, and went in the strength of
that food forty days and nights to Horeb the mount of God. (1
Kings 19:7-8)

Don't you wish you had access to the recipe for that
coal-baked cake? Caffeine-induced spurts of energy just
don't measure up to divinely inspired get-up-and-go!

Where did God want Elijah to go? To Mt. Horeb, the

mount of God—another name for Mt. Sinai, where the Law had been given to Moses. As we have learned, there is another association with Mt. Horeb. This was the place where Moses had smitten the rock with the rod of God, and Jehovah-nissi had caused water to gush forth to quench the people's thirst.

MT. HOREB—RENDEZVOUS WITH GOD

El Roi was taking Elijah back to a historic spot to rejuvenate him with the water of life. To give him once again a desire to live. To rid him of his anger and frustration.

To help him realize that the abundant life springs only from God Himself—not fireworks, not waterworks, not dynamic displays of power, but from the Creator of all of these.

Mt. Horeb had also been the setting for the reunion of Moses and his wife Zipporah, who was brought to him by her father, Jethro. When Jethro saw that his son-in-law was overworked, he suggested that Moses give up trying to settle everyone's problems and designate responsibility to "God-fearing men of truth" (Exod. 18:21) who would judge the people and bring only the "Supreme Court" cases to Moses.

A similar message awaited Elijah at Mt. Horeb. But first El Roi made sure that the tired prophet was completely alone, away from all human distraction and persuasion. Elijah's second cross-country marathon had a strange place of completion—a cave.

Perhaps not so strange to some of us! I've often experienced a "cave mentality," when I've wanted to retreat from society and hide from every human eye—and telephone. (I must admit that I like my caves to be free of snakes and spiders, preferably with a nice view and lots of light for reading.)

The God who sees was watching Elijah.

"And, behold, the word of the Lord came and He said to him, What are you doing here, Elijah?" (1 Kings 19:9).

Somehow there's the sense of the parent finding a child, thumb in mouth, sitting in a hidden corner. The parent tries not to laugh as he asks: "What in the world are you doing here?"

Elijah was extremely defensive:

I have been very jealous for the Lord God of hosts; for the Israelites have forsaken Your covenant, thrown down Your altars, and killed Your prophets with the sword; and I, I only, am left; and they seek my life, to take it away. (1 Kings 19:10)

El Roi didn't argue with Elijah. He didn't condemn him for hiding. He simply encouraged him to come out of the cave and to "stand on the mount before the Lord" (1 Kings 19:11).

Perhaps you, like Elijah, have experienced emotional and physical burn-out, and you headed for a cave. I remember times when I holed up in an emotional cave because I was painfully embarrassed by the actions of a family member. Then there were times when I felt like a complete failure because of a work situation or when I couldn't cope with what seemed like prying questions.

I vividly remember not wanting to talk to *one more person* after my mother's death.

Some of these reactions, like those of grief, simply take time to heal—several weeks, months, or even years to sort out. In other examples of cave mentality, however, the initial problem gets worse the longer the cave-dweller hides.

Sometimes repressed anger forces us into a cave, a cave that eventually walls us into a dungeon of depression.

If we will allow Him to, El Roi leads us out of our caves, out onto the "mountain of God," where we can hear His voice.

THE STILL, SMALL VOICE

And behold, the Lord passed by, and a great and strong wind
rent the mountains, and broke in pieces the rocks before the
Lord, but the Lord was not in the wind; and after the wind an
earthquake, but the Lord was not in the earthquake;
   And after the earthquake a fire, but the Lord was not in the
fire; and after the fire [a sound of gentle stillness and] a still,
small voice.
   When Elijah heard the voice, he wrapped his face in his
mantle and went out and stood in the entrance of the cave. And
behold, there came a voice to him, and said, What are you doing
here, Elijah? (1 Kings 19:11-13)

   Again, the defense:

I have been very jealous for the Lord God of hosts; because the
Israelites have forsaken Your covenant, thrown down Your
altars, and slain Your prophets with the sword; and I, I only,
am left, and they seek my life, to destroy it. (1 Kings 19:14)

   And again, El Roi did not argue or condemn. He had a
simple solution for Elijah's exhaustion, for his loneliness,
for his depression.
   God spoke firmly: "Listen to My directions. Accept My
plans. Realize that I am in control—not only of your life
but also of all Israel and even of Syria. Accept the fact that
you need help and train Elisha to assist you and eventually
replace you. You are not alone. And you are replaceable. I
am El Elyon, the Most High God."
   God gave specific directions:

Go, return . . . anoint Hazael to be king over Syria [Ahab
would be attacked by Hazael] . . . anoint Jehu son of Nimshi to
be king over Israel [Jehu was a strong opponent of Baal-worship]
. . . anoint Elisha son of Shaphat of Abel-meholah to be prophet

in your place [Elisha would continue the spiritual war]. (1 Kings 19:15-16)

El Roi was aware of the problems; He had planned an inward and an outward purge of Israel. And El Elyon was in control.

Before Elijah could absorb that assurance, however, he had to do three things. First, he had to rest. Then he had to get to the mount of God, the place where he knew God could be found. And finally he had to come out of his cave and listen to God's voice.

Somehow we lust for the dynamics of the fireworks, the mighty wind, the attention-getting earthquakes. But God's ultimate answer is given in a still, small voice.

The voice we can hear only after our ears have adjusted to the gentle quiet of God's presence.

Therein lies the answer to our anger, our expectations of ourselves and others, our disillusionment with human imperfection.

Several months ago I received a letter from a young, single, lonely, tired missionary. Carol had been battling the feeling that God was no longer speaking to her. She was very much in need of a time of rest. I quote from her letter, with her permission.

I began to think about why I felt that He had not been speaking to me. I began to think that perhaps I was expecting or demanding something and thus missing out on what He actually was doing. I wanted Him to speak to me in some way out of the ordinary. It dawned on me then that that kind of attitude prevented me from fully appreciating those moments when He did speak through others or through simple everyday events.

This is what I thought about while camping out in the mountains for four days. They were beautiful days beside one of the loveliest lakes I know. As I looked at the crystal-clear water and watched the sun climb up over the mountains and asked the Lord to restore tranquillity, I thought about how often I missed

*hearing His voice because of wanting to hear it in a different
way.*

*Those four days were good days of rest—not nearly enough,
but the beginning. . . . The thought of "ministry" doesn't excite
me yet, a sign that I'm not fully restored. But one thing I
know—that will pass and I'll come out alright.*

*Time is a wonderful thing in God's hands, and He is doing
and will continue to do His work.*

Carol

Just this week I received another letter from the "lonely,
tired missionary." She now described herself as "one scared
missionary"—for good reason! With two native couples,
she is involved in planting a new church, beginning a
totally new outreach in the city where she lives. The
depression I read between the lines in earlier letters has
been replaced by enthusiasm; what seemed like inevitable
breakdown or a desire for breakaway is becoming
breakthrough!

El Roi sees. El Elyon is all-powerful. The God of
prevision is also the God of provision . . . in His time.

WHAT IS THE MEANING OF HIS NAME?

1. Why do some people assume that all anger—and any
expression of it—is sinful? Discuss Proverbs 19:19; 27:2-6,
15-17.

2. Discuss the implications of the warning given in
Ephesians 6:4. Could anger be one of the "sins of the
fathers" (Num. 14:18) that leaves its mark as far as the
third and fourth generations?

3. In addition to writing, what methods of constructively
dealing with anger can you cite? How do *you* express
anger?

4. What are questions we should ask ourselves when we
feel anger?

5. How does Ephesians 4:26 give direction in handling anger? Why is it so important to take care of anger in the right way? Discuss Hebrews 12:14-15.

6. Against whom is it possible for the perfectionist to unconsciously direct anger?

7. Using the following passages, differentiate between human anger and divine anger or "wrath": Isaiah 14:1-8; 54:4-8; Habakkuk 3:2-8. How did God deal with His anger against sin? (See Isa. 53:5-6, 11-12.) What does Isaiah 13:6-11 say about God's future wrath?

8. Describe the contrast between the meanings of El Roi and El Elyon. Why is it important to keep both meanings in mind?

9. What had to happen in Elijah's life before he could absorb the assurance in these meanings of God's names?

9

Why Do I Feel Like an Orphan?

EL SHADDAI:
The mighty One who is
also the tender comforter

Janet and Marie met in a continuing education class. Janet was married and had two children. Marie lived by herself, hundreds of miles away from her family. She was obviously lonely.

Janet liked Marie and wanted to be her friend, but when they spent time together she felt overwhelmed by Marie's compliments and developing possessiveness. Janet allowed the relationship to continue, but she began to feel more and more boxed in.

Finally Janet expressed her feelings to Marie. The conversation was extremely difficult for both women, and for some time afterward Marie avoided Janet. Janet regretted the hurt she had brought on but knew she had done the right thing. When Marie went home for a vacation, Janet felt as though a burden had been lifted from her shoulders. Up to that point, she had not realized how much stress the situation had presented.

Janet continued to pray for Marie. When a letter arrived in the mail one day, Janet read it anxiously. Here it is, with Janet and Marie's permission.

Dear Janet,

First, I want to thank you for what you've done for me. Let me take this time to remind you.

After you called me that day on the phone, I thought I'd explode. So many feelings were going on inside me. You told me you thought I was depending on you for too much in our relationship. You felt I was wanting you to fulfill my emotional needs and not God.

In a loving way you told me I needed to branch out and make more friends, instead of looking to you as much as I did. Then you listed several of the qualities that made me a good friend.

It was all for my own good. I realized that later. But I sure didn't feel that way then. It was necessary for you to tell me what you did. I knew that even then. But I wanted to scream, cry, and hit someone at the same time. You had very gently cut the apron strings, but your "baby" didn't think she could survive for long without you. You had no intentions of ending our friendship, but I didn't realize that then. I was ready to just move out of the area so I wouldn't have to face seeing you at classes and not be able to talk to you.

I didn't call on my heavenly Father to fill my emotional needs at that time. Even though He was there, and you and He both wanted me to trust Him. . . .

But I did survive and I did grow. Gradually I made other friends and began to call on God more. I even got close to a couple of people without depending on them emotionally. I was quite pleased with my efforts. I thought I was doing well.

Some time ago I met Priscilla. After I'd known her a few weeks, I told her about the problems I'd had and expressed the fact that I did not want to become emotionally dependent on her. She agreed we needed to watch for that. Then she went to school and I didn't see her for awhile. I was daily asking God to help me to trust Him more and to fill my needs.

I saw Priscilla over a weekend again and then she went back to school.

A couple weeks later I lost it completely. It was as if I'd been

totally abandoned by God. One night I just took a walk at nine
o'clock in ten-degree weather and yelled at Him.

My conversation went something like this: "You promised me
You'd fill all of my needs. So why don't you fill this one? I don't
mind being alone sometimes. But what am I supposed to do
when I want someone just to be there, someone to talk to? All the
mature, stable friends You've provided me with are married,
with a family. They love me. But they can't always be there
when I need them.

"I know . . . I'm supposed to call on You. I know You hear
me. But, as the kids say, I want someone with skin on! Someone
to hold me when I cry, someone to tell me they care. Not someone
who has to rush home to fix supper for the family just when I
need them most.

"It obviously isn't Your desire to send me a husband. So who
do I turn to? The younger friends I have that are single want
what I can give them, but don't have the ability to give back to
me what I need. So what am I supposed to do, God?"

Janet . . . God didn't answer me. Do you have any answers?
I know the life of married people isn't a bed of roses either. Their
spouse isn't always there to fulfill their needs, or they simply
don't have it in them to. No one person can fill all your needs.

But at least a spouse is there more than my few close friends
are with me. I try to combat being lonely by helping someone
who is worse off than I am. But you can't always give and give.

I know I must trust God to fill my emotional needs. But why
does something still seem to be missing? Why doesn't He seem to
be there when I need Him the most?

Marie

How can Marie's questions be answered? And what
about Janet's feelings? What should we do when we reach
out in love to someone, only to become entangled in a tight
web of hurt emotions?

In today's world the word "love" is used loosely; it has a
variety of definitions. But God's kind of love involves

responsibility. Love means committing oneself to a relationship, listening as well as talking, weeping together as well as rejoicing.

Love—this vague, quivery, good-to-the-senses-emotion—is not love at all until it gels into commitment.

Love = CIA. Love is commitment in action.

But there is another point to consider. It is important to discern when the self*less*ness that is so much a part of love becomes futile sacrifice at the shrine of another's self*ish*ness. God blesses commitment, but He does not expect us to lose our identities through confused loyalties.

"EL SHADDAI HAS DEALT BITTERLY WITH ME . . ."

The story of Ruth and Naomi beautifully illustrates this truth. Imagine with me Naomi's feelings as she is stranded in a strange country, Moab, after the death of her husband and two sons:

Alone . . . alone . . . I feel so all alone.
There's no one here to understand
The way I feel. My heart cries out
For someone who can fill the empty spot
My husband's death has left.

Call me no longer by the name Naomi—
That name belonged to happier days than these—
But call me Mara now . . . my life is bitter.
Yes, God Almighty has dealt bitterly with me.
I went out from this country full;
My husband and my sons walked by my side,
But God has sent me back again, my quiver empty,
With none but Ruth to ease the awful pain inside. [1]

Years after that poem was written, I learned that the original Hebrew words for God Almighty, to whom Naomi referred, were *El Shaddai.* As we discussed in chapter 2, El

Shaddai is the One who fills and makes fruitful, the God who bestows the blessing of the breast to the fruit of the womb.

To review, *Shaddai*, derived from the Hebrew word *shad* (breast), suggests the tenderness of a nursing mother who brings comfort to her child in the night. *El* carries the connotation of strength and power.

But Naomi says:

Call me not Naomi [pleasant], call me Mara [bitter]; for the Almighty has dealt very bitterly with me. I went out full, and the Lord has brought me home again empty; why call me Naomi, since the Lord has testified against me, and the Almighty [El Shaddai] has afflicted me? (Ruth 1:20-21)

Naomi cannot understand why the all-powerful One has not kept this calamity from coming upon her.

Have you ever felt like Naomi?

Naomi and her husband had come to Moab because of famine in Israel; now, however, she hears that in her hometown Bethlehem, which means "the house of bread," food is again plentiful. She decides to return to Bethlehem, but advises her Moabite daughters-in-law to stay in their homeland, where it is more likely that they will find husbands again.

One daughter-in-law, Orpah, wavers in her decision but finally chooses the easier option. Ruth, whose name means "friendship," chooses the unselfish alternative:

Entreat me not to leave thee,
or to return from following after thee:
for whither thou goest,
I will go;
and where thou lodgest,
I will lodge:
thy people shall be my people,
and thy God my God. (Ruth 1:16, KJV).

That's commitment! That's what love is all about!

Ruth and Naomi return to Bethlehem together, and Ruth continues to serve Naomi unselfishly by going out to glean grain in the fields. Their relationship, however, is not a one-way street. Naomi's life has been touched by Ruth's selflessness, and she responds in kind. Naomi "seeks rest" for her daughter-in-law through marriage to Naomi's kinsman Boaz, whose name means "strength." Boaz marries Ruth and presents Naomi with a new purpose in life—Naomi becomes the "nanny" to her grandson Obed. His name, meaning "born to serve," seems a fitting summary of Ruth's life.

El Shaddai turns our miseries into ministries. The misery of Mara becomes the natal song of Naomi:

Who could have known the Lord's intentions
When things seemed only to be going wrong?
Who could have known I'd nurse a baby
And in my heart there'd ring a song?
Boaz and Ruth have been to me a family;
My daughter-in-law is better than ten sons!
Her love has taken me through sorrow
And proved to me once more that God is love.[2]

REPRESENTING EL SHADDAI

Let's be realistic. Not all relationships end as happily as Ruth and Naomi's. Not all same-sex relationships are helpful to both people involved.

I vividly remember my mother telling me in hushed tones about a roommate from nurses' training. This friend had offered to work and provide financial support in exchange for a lesbian relationship if my mother would "keep house." Mother's reaction was one of horror!

That experience came from the 1920s; today's tones are no longer hushed. The AIDS epidemic has made homosexuality a household word. But in many homes the reactions are still similar to my mother's. Unfortunately, relationships may be severely threatened or even destroyed by overtones or fears of homosexuality. Sadly enough, members of the Christian community may even avoid involvement with singles or singles' groups because of suspicions of homosexuality.

Please understand my intention in discussing homosexuality. I want to encourage members of the body of Christ to differentiate between legitimate emotional needs and actual homosexual behavior—and, in either case, to act as representatives of El Shaddai.

I am convinced that the formation of homosexual patterns of behavior often could be prevented if members of the Christian community understood the underlying causes. In many cases, social patterns of our day—especially the rising rate of divorce—create the seedbeds of homosexual behavior.

Colin Cook, an ex-homosexual who with his wife is now involved in a ministry to homosexuals, Quest Learning Center, P.O. Box 7881, Reading, PA 19603 (215-376-1146) published an informative booklet entitled *Homosexuality: An Open Door?* In it, he quoted an English author, Elizabeth Moberly, whose writing is extremely helpful in understanding the homosexual development pattern.

Moberly commented:

From amidst a welter of details, one constant underlying principle suggests itself: that the homosexual—whether man or woman—has suffered from some deficit in the relationship with the parent of the same sex; and that there is a corresponding drive to make good this deficit—through the medium of same-sex or "homosexual" relationships.

In speaking of a deficit, it must be stressed that this does not always imply willful maltreatment by the parent in question, as distinct from unintentional or accidental hurt. But in every case, it is postulated, something of a traumatic nature, whether ill-treatment, neglect, or sheer absence, has in these particular instances led to a disruption in the normal attachment. This in turn implies that psychological needs that are normally met through the child's attachment to the parent are left unfulfilled. [3]

A strong need for same-sex relationships, therefore, may be an expression of a person's unfulfilled need for a loving relationship with the parent of the same sex. If somewhere in childhood this relationship was cut off, either because of physical absence or emotional distance on the part of the parent, the child may have been severely hurt in the process.

Whether this happened intentionally or involuntarily, the child may have built an emotional wall between himself and the parent—a "defensive detachment," as Moberly described it. This wall signified a lack of trust and therefore a decision, whether conscious or unconscious, not to receive love from that parent in the future.

The love-gap remains, however, and needs to be filled. The child inside the adult continues to search for a relationship with someone to fill the gap. Naturally, the relationship must be with someone of the same sex.

In her book on homosexuality entitled *The Broken Image,* Leanne Payne of Pastoral Care Ministries in Milwaukee, Wisconsin, commented: "As a sexual neurosis, lesbian behavior is not nearly so complicated as male homosexual behavior. Most that I have seen and worked with is rooted in a need for a mother's arms, a need that was never or only insufficiently met."[4]

Tragically, in the sinful world in which we live, emotional needs are constantly eroticized. An emotionally deprived adult, confused by yearnings for parental love, may conclude that because this yearning is for members of the same sex it must be homosexual in nature.

Filled with bewilderment and shame, this person may cut herself off from close relationships with others in an effort to control her lust, which is not actually lust, but a yearning for a relationship with a loving mother.

At precisely this time, mature, caring members of the body of Christ can "fill the gap" and become family to the hurt and hurting individual. We can represent to her the El Shaddai we find described in Isaiah 66:12-13:

For thus says the Lord . . . then you shall be nursed, you shall be trotted on her hip, and be trotted on her [God's maternal] knees.
As one whom his mother comforts, so will I comfort you. . . .

If a young woman can find a fulfilling relationship with an older woman in the church—writer Miriam Neff talks about the need for a "Titus woman"—that relationship may be the catalyst that gradually transforms her into an emotional adult.[5]

HOW THE CYCLE BEGINS

Perhaps, however, this young woman feels rejected or misunderstood by people within the church. Worse yet, perhaps she is confirmed in her suspicions of homosexuality by another person struggling with similar feelings. Eventually, homosexual activity may result.

Consequently, confusion may turn into the conviction that "I was born a homosexual." Homosexual activity may develop into a pattern, a vicious cycle of yearning for affection and being confirmed by the wrong sources in the wrong way rather than by the body of Christ.

Counseling for women who struggle with homosexual feelings is a must. Christian counselors can help women realize that strands of "evidence," such as homosexual dreams, are inadequate indicators of the need for an "alternate life-style." Andy Comiskey, whose Desert Stream ministry weekly counsels more than seventy women and men who struggle with homosexuality, commented: "In light of current research, we can say that sexual identity spurs more from one's learning and environment than hormonal or chromosomal imbalances."[6]

Complicating the feelings of a struggling homosexual is the difficulty of forgiving the same-sex parent. Often the decision not to receive love from that parent was a preadult decision, in some cases dating from very early years. As a result, much hurt and resentment is unconscious and therefore difficult to deal with. There is a deep inability to trust the parent, who represents a source of love that was experienced as hurtful. This inability to trust may transfer to other people who are honestly trying to accept and help—or to the concept of a Father-God.

All of this needs to be understood by those of us who attempt to touch the hurting with Christ's love. We must learn not to jump to conclusions, not to categorize people, not to judge by appearances—and not to take the place of God as people begin to trust us and depend on us.

There is so much more that could be said on this topic. Take advantage of the reading material that is available.[7] Be aware of the needs around you, and be ready to use your special gifts of ministry—encouragement, comfort, exhortation, or helps—as God leads you.

A DEPENDENT MUST BECOME AN ADULT

Another factor must be considered. I correspond with a young mother, Sue, whose marriage had been subtly undermined by a working relationship with a young woman I'll call Nancy. Nancy had been involved in homosexual activity. Although she was trying to put the past behind her, her friendship with Sue, who was trying to help her, drained Sue emotionally and created tension in her marriage.

Finally, after much prayer, Sue decided she needed to break off the relationship with Nancy. She realized that her "times of praise and prayer" with Nancy had interfered with her spiritual relationship with her husband and prevented him from becoming the spiritual leader in the home. Eventually Nancy and Sue stopped meeting so that each could move on in the direction the Lord was calling her. Sue wrote:

Since that time I feel as if a dam has broken and all the living water it had been holding back has now been freed to flow. My husband didn't say so at first, but I know this decision was a relief to him. He's always been a little dubious about Nancy's feelings for me and a little threatened by the spiritual relationship I had gotten so much from. He's very much in need of several years of particularly undivided devotion, and I'm finally getting the ears and heart to understand this.

So until the Lord says to resume a relationship with Nancy, we are not in touch with each other at all. I have a feeling, from what she shared initially, that this has been more painful for her than for me. But I know it's all a part of the tremendous work He's doing in her life with relationships. He's freeing her to get on with her calling without any extra baggage, particularly any kind of a dependency on me. For myself, it is a relief to be at peace with God's plan for centering in and refining this marriage, and all my impatience has disintegrated in the realization that there are some basics to take care of first.

Let's close this chapter with one final illustration from life—the story of David and Jonathan. Some would like to categorize this relationship as homosexual because of David's statement that Jonathan's love was "wonderful, passing the love of women" (2 Sam. 1:26).

Taking this statement in context, however, we realize that Jonathan was the brother of Michal, David's first wife. Michal was given to David by her father, King Saul, as a reward for David's killing of 1,000 enemy Philistines. Although she was loyal in helping David escape from Saul, later—while David was hiding in the wilderness for three years to escape Saul's anger—Michal was married to another man, Phalti. When David was crowned king, the new monarch demanded that Michal return to him; she did so, but with her loving husband following her, weeping.

Had Michal given her heart to Phalti—or only her hand, under duress? Scripture does not tell us, but she did show a lack of love for David when she expressed disgust at his dancing in the streets during a religious processional.

In contrast, Jonathan's love for David was ever faithful. He was not jealous of David's popularity; rather, he assured David of their future together, in reversed roles: "You are going to be the king of Israel and I will be next to you, as my father is well aware" (1 Sam. 23:17, TLB).

Jonathan did more than reassure David of their friendship. Taking a chance of incurring his father's wrath by meeting David in the forest, "and strengthened his hand in God" (1 Sam. 23:16, KJV).

DETACH AND ATTACH—TO EL SHADDAI

Notice how wisely Jonathan handled this precious but precarious relationship. He did not comfort David so much that his friendship became *necessary* to David, that David could not survive without him. He visited his friend and then left him—but left him strong and confident in God.

As Amy Carmichael says so beautifully, "he detaches his dear David from himself and attaches him to his 'very present help.'"[8]

The next time David encountered serious problems, there was no Jonathan to help him find strength in God. "And David was greatly distressed; for the people spoke of stoning him . . . *but David encouraged himself in the Lord his God*" (1 Sam. 30:6, KJV, emphasis mine).

If he had leaned on Jonathan, if Jonathan had made himself necessary to David, [David] would not have leaned on his Rock and proved the glorious strength of his Rock; his whole life would have been lived on a lower level, and who can tell how many of his songs would have been left unwritten, with great loss to the glory of God and to the Church of all the ages.

So let us not weaken those whom we love by weak sympathy, but let us love them enough to detach them from ourselves and strengthen their hands in God. [9]

God has put within us the urge to interact with other human beings. He has provided relationships to supply the security and encouragement we humans so desperately need. But Satan has devised a subtle trap. A dependency on a human relationship can hold us back from experiencing the ultimate relationship.

We have found that God's power is matched by His tenderness. The name El Shaddai expresses the richness and fullness of God's grace, which poured itself out for others in self-sacrificing love. His strength is made perfect in our weakness; His sufficiency is most manifest in our insufficiency.

Perhaps as we begin to understand the two-pronged nature of El Shaddai—His tenderness as well as His power—more of us will spend time translating the tenderness of that power to a hurting, needy world.

Translating it through committing our lives, not just mouthing words.

WHAT IS THE MEANING OF HIS NAME?

1. How does the meaning of the word *Shaddai* balance the meaning of *El?*

2. A fruit tree requires cutting back in order to bear fruit most efficiently. El Shaddai prunes as well as blesses His people so that they will bear spiritual fruits. How did this process occur in the story of Ruth and Naomi? What may be a result of pruning, as expressed in John 15:2?

3. Define the meanings of the following names: Bethlehem, Ruth, Naomi, Mara, Boaz, Obed.

4. Why has the relationship between David and Jonathan been called homosexual? What happened to David's relationship with Michal, the sister of Jonathan? How might this have influenced his comment about Jonathan's loyal love? In later years, after Jonathan's death, how did David continue to evidence his concern for the house of Jonathan? (See 2 Sam. 9:1-13.)

5. What does Elizabeth Moberly see as the one constant that underlies a homosexual orientation? How might this constant relate to the meaning of Numbers 14:18? How can the cycle be broken?

6. In Moberly's scenario, is disruption in the parent-child relationship necessarily intentional? Why is forgiveness so difficult? Describe a defensive detachment and give an example you have experienced or witnessed.

7. How many women in your congregation fit the description in Titus 2:3-5? Perhaps God could use *you* as a "Titus woman." From Titus 2, does it sound as though women who reach retirement age have no value in the church? On the side of caution, how can a marriage be undermined when either partner is overinvolved in a same-sex relationship—even when there is no homosexual activity involved?

10

*How Can God Want
to Associate with Me?*

JEHOVAH-M'KADDESH:
The God who sanctifies
JEHOVAH-TSIDKENU:
The righteous One

I felt physically and emotionally drained from the retreat. I had spent an entire afternoon listening to Linda, a woman who told me she "felt like a freak"; she was sure she was the only one in her church who had come from such a "weird" background. Ironically, other women from her church told me they thought she had it all together—looks, figure, beautiful home, successful husband. What more could she ask for?

The women in Linda's church had no idea that Linda had been a victim of incest. They were unable to help her.

I had listened—but had I helped her?

Should I even have mentioned the subject in my message at the retreat? Had I caused more hurt than healing? Why couldn't I make people laugh instead of cry? Why had God placed this burden on me?

The day's mail brought an answer:

Dear Joy,
I was at the retreat where you spoke and am led to write you for several reasons. The first thing I want to say is thank you for saying God's words.

I need to share my story with you. I was molested by both of my brothers for many years when they were "babysitting" for my parents. I hated them so much and I hated my parents and, although I didn't know Him then, I hated God too.

I am the only believer in my family at this time and it has been hard to forgive [my brothers] and be a good example. I have finally forgiven most of my family members. Certainly I love God and have learned to accept His love. I still experience anxiety with one of my brothers, though. I've learned that healing comes slowly. It was locked inside of me for over ten years until after I came to know God, so I know I can't just expect to snap my fingers and have it go away.

I was heavily involved in drugs until I became a believer. It was the easiest way to pretend that [incest] never happened.

God's love has been enveloping me for five years and He has given me many special friends who have tried to understand, but how can you really if you've never experienced it yourself?

I still don't like men very much at all. That makes me feel so abnormal. I was so scared for so many years that I was a lesbian or at least extremely abnormal. I am anxiously awaiting the day when I can minister as you do and finally can say God and I have overcome.

*I have read David Seamands's books (*Healing of Memories *and* Healing for Damaged Emotions*). They have helped me so and I am continually suggesting them to others. I read constantly to help me heal. I cannot bring myself to go to a counselor again. (I went once or twice.) It is just too difficult.*

I write poetry and would like to share one of my poems with you.

We're here for each other;
It's in God's perfect plan.
Jesus showed us how when He was a man.

We're here for each other;
It's plain to see
Sometimes I need you and sometimes you need me.

We're here for each other;
Without a doubt
That's what our lives are all about.

We're here for each other
To share God's love
Until we are with Him in heaven above.

Joy, you have helped me just by being open. Thank you again.
In our Savior's precious love,

Stacey

Several weeks later I received a ten-page letter from Linda, echoing the need for openness and acceptance, for reassurance that victims are not alone in their terrible memories, that they are not freaks.

Linda has found a professional counselor—someone, by the way, who has experienced the same hurt and is now free to become a healed helper.

Sometimes the Holy Spirit alone becomes our private Counselor as well as our Comforter. This was the case with Mary, a gentle lady who talked to me after a mother-daughter banquet at which I spoke. She confided in me that she had been a childhood victim of incest, then wrote to me later that evening.

Thank you again for your message tonight. I shared with you something no one else in the world knows except those who abused me and my dear Savior. Why I shared it, I do not know, except it touched me so to hear someone telling those precious ones in the same situation that they do not have to carry all that guilt.

How often it should be told today in all churches! It seems to me that even the pastors should be saying it from the pulpit, but nothing is ever said.

Thank you again.

In Jesus,
Mary

156 When God Seems Far Away

Mary was one of the most beautiful senior citizens I have ever met. Her face was gentle and unscarred; it did not show a trace of bitterness. She had shared her secret only with Jesus, and He had healed the wound.

Mary is typical of many incest victims in that she had never disclosed her childhood experiences. She is not typical, however, in other ways.

Because of their crippling guilt and reluctance to tell someone else, many victims never find healing.

In an excellent article entitled "Incest: The Family Secret," an author who has chosen to remain anonymous for the sake of rebuilding family relationships speaks authoritatively from personal experience:

Sexual abuse happens in families of every social, economic, and ethnic background—not just among the poor and unreligious. . . . One girl out of four and one boy out of ten will be sexually assaulted at least once by the age of eighteen—and for those trapped in the nightmare of incest, the average period of abuse is seven years. . . . In recent years, 70 percent of the prison inmates and 90 percent of the prostitutes interviewed had been molested as children.

In its strictest definition, incest is sexual intercourse between people who are too closely related to marry. It also includes other sexual acts such as molestation, fondling, and exhibitionism, since these too leave deep and lasting emotional scars. . . .

Physical force or severe threats are rarely needed to take advantage of children or [to] keep them from telling. Though innocent, they feel dirty, ashamed, and "different," sensing the wrongness of the situation. . . . Shame and fear work together to keep a stranglehold on a child's ability to call out for help.

When a child does get up enough courage to tell someone, many times their parents or friends respond to their claim with horror, disbelief, judgment, or denial.

All abuse victims struggle with shame, false guilt, and a horrible distortion of self-worth. [1]

AN AGE-OLD PROBLEM

Incest is an age-old problem. It is mentioned twice in Genesis and also in 2 Samuel. Perpetrators of incest have justified their actions by insisting: "It has *always* happened—it's in the Bible."

The first incident recorded in Scripture, Genesis 19:30-38, involves a drunken Lot and his young and restless daughters. In this case, incest was actually initiated by the daughters in an effort to continue the race, which became the nation of Moab. The family had fled the burning city of Sodom, but not before they had been brainwashed by its slogan: "Anything goes!"

As you may remember, Lot had chosen Sodom and "the well-watered plain" of Jordan when allowed to make the decision by his uncle Abraham. Years later, he made another disastrous choice when he offered his virgin daughters to the bestiality of the Sodomites—all in an effort to protect his male visitors who were actually angels and certainly not in need of Lot's protection. His daughters, who *did* need his protection, must have lost any respect they might have had for their father that fateful night in Sodom. They became driven, manipulative women.

Two other stories of incest in the Bible involved two women named Tamar. The Tamar of Genesis 38, strangely enough, also initiated the relationship between herself and her father-in-law. Her purpose was to prove his injustice and hypocrisy, and she collected her evidence, as shrewdly as any lawyer.[2]

On the significance of the story of Tamar, Eugenia Price writes:

We err when we try to find "lessons" in all these Old Testament accounts. They are not little "morality plays." They are records, historical records, however sketchy at times, of the lives of some of the people of Israel and their friends and enemies. We are not to try to be like them or not to be like them. We are to look for what God did in all they did. *We are to look for what God did directly, at the time of their behavior or misbehavior, and in this story we are to look also for what He dared to do later. All through the twilight era of the Old Testament, God was planning, moving toward the day when He would send His Son Jesus, to redeem His people from their sins. To give them a way to live fully, abundantly without tricks or devices such as Tamar used.*

This is the exciting, overwhelming, humbling message of the somewhat risqué story of the beautiful Tamar: God sent His Son through her!

One author said it shocked his "inner, finer feelings to see Christ's lineage interwoven with such abhorrent degradation. . . ." It definitely does not shock mine. It relieves me all the way to the depths of my soul to see that the Holy God of Israel loved enough to make use of ordinary people. . . .

This is the Most High God striding across the earth shouting, "I love! I love! You cannot achieve holiness. Nothing you can do by way of morality can bring us together. By grace are you saved."[3]

THE DESOLATE VICTIM

The story of the second Tamar, the daughter of King David, is heartrending in its realism. After witnessing the adulterous relationship between David and Bathsheba, the king's son Amnon forced his half-sister Tamar into an incestuous relationship.

Her words of protest echo the screams of many other innocent victims: "No! My brother, do not force and humble me, for no such thing should be done in Israel! Do not do this foolhardy, scandalous thing! And I, how could I rid myself of my shame?" (2 Sam. 13:12-13).

But Amnon would not listen.

Being stronger than she, he forced her, and lay with her. Then Amnon hated her exceedingly; so that his hatred for her was

greater than the love with which he had loved her. And Amnon
said to her, Get up, and get out!
   But she said, No! This great evil of sending me away is worse
than what you did to me. But he would not listen to her.
   He called the servant who served him, and said, Put this
woman out of my presence, now, and bolt the door after her!
(2 Sam. 13:14-17)

A book entitled *Betrayal of Innocence* was written by
authors who may or may not have heard the story of
Tamar and Amnon, but their comments on sibling incest
are pertinent:

The . . . older-brother aggressor, several years older than his
younger sister, tends to be a disturbed individual before the
incest begins. He is like the father-aggressor who uses incest as a
means of trying to cope with unconscious needs and conflicts.
This older brother is usually intimidated by women. . . . He
finds his little sister's passivity nonthreatening.[4]

The authors also discussed incest between siblings close
to the same age, pointing out that although this type of
situation is not considered nearly as emotionally dangerous
as the older brother-younger sister relationship, the
participants—especially the brother—may still live with
tremendous guilt.
   Certainly Amnon, in the biblical account, showed
definite signs of emotional disturbance, and just as certainly
his actions pierced deep wounds into Tamar's fragile self-
esteem. Note the vivid descriptiveness of the story:

Now [Tamar] was wearing a long robe with sleeves and of
various colors, for in such robes were the king's virgin daughters
clad of old.
   Then Amnon's servant brought her out, and bolted the door
after her. And [she] put ashes on her head, and tore the long,

*sleeved robe which she wore, and she laid her hand on her head,
and went away shrieking and wailing. (2 Sam. 13:18-19)*

Who listened to Tamar's screams? "And Absalom her
brother said to her, 'Has your brother Amnon been with
you? Be quiet now, my sister. He is your brother; take not
this matter to heart'" (2 Sam. 13:20).

Absalom did, however, attempt to avenge his sister by
murdering their half-brother Amnon. But revenge did not
heal the wound. The final sentence of the passage is tragic.
"So Tamar dwelt in her brother Absalom's house, a
desolate woman."

In all the biblical versions I checked, that same word—
"desolate"—was used in reference to Tamar. Perhaps no
other word better describes the victim of incest. *Webster's
New World Dictionary of the American Language* defines the
word "desolate" as "left alone, lonely, solitary; uninhabited,
deserted; made uninhabitable, laid waste, in a ruinous
state; forlorn, wretched."

An unnamed victim emphasizes:

*Incest is much, much more than the violation of a child's body.
It's the ultimate betrayal of their trust in the very people who are
supposed to be their protectors, comforters, and closest friends.
While they are suffering the most severe form of emotional abuse,
their loyalty and love for their abuser make it nearly impossible
for them to speak up.* [5]

And so a woman may remain desolate, as Tamar did,
living with the aftereffects of incest for the rest of her life.

DANCE OF DEATH

In the New Testament, incest is suggested in the story of the
daughter of Herodias, who was named Salome by the
historian Josephus. To please her power-hungry mother,
Salome performed a dance, traditionally known as the

"Dance of the Seven Veils," before Herod Antipas and his court.

Could I know why my mother asked
I dance for Herod? 'Twas her wish!
I shrank from facing his eyes too,
Avoided his fond father's kiss.
I hated him with all my heart
And yet enjoyed the lust he showed,
Felt flattered by his compliments,
Wanted to show my womanhood.[6]

Salome's sensual dance became a dance of death for John the Baptist and perhaps a similar sentence for her as well—a death to innocence. The Herodian family was full of incestuous marriages. Later young Salome married her great-uncle, Herod Philip II.

Tragically, Herodias is not alone as a mother who encouraged her daughter into a "dance of death." Herodias is one among many who, for varying reasons, have betrayed their own flesh and blood.

I'VE BEEN USED!

Shame and guilt, as we have mentioned, are almost inevitable effects of incest. Nan, a dear friend who has survived incest, sent me an outline of a lecture she presented at a girls' home on this all-too-familiár topic. The outline listed other emotional aftereffects of incest.

According to Nan, the victim of incest feels the need to be "super-adaptable." Her multifaceted personality, however, is an "act" at which she has become adept, having learned to play the game of whatever "he"—her father or another male—wanted her to be: "perhaps a baseball player, possibly a cook, perhaps a source of strength."

This act extends into future relationships with other

men, men who offer acceptance which is seen by the victim of incest as love. Because of her low self-image, the victim may settle for whatever source of attention she can find, often with disastrous effects.

The girl's (or woman's) sense of worthlessness may show up in mood swings, depression, dependence on others, or possessiveness. A cycle of weight gain and diet pills may ensue, often leading to the use of drugs ("to blot out the pain and to self-destruct") or alcohol ("to quit hurting and forget the guilt"). Self-mutilation may be a victim's desperate signal for attention, a way to deal with anger and resentment. ("We were taught that we don't get mad at our parents, so we take it out on ourselves or others.") Unmet cries for help may lead to more attention-getting devices or serious attempts at suicide.

HOPE FOR HEALING

Can the wounds imposed by incest ever be healed? Is it possible to recover from this severe form of physical, emotional, and spiritual abuse?

Certainly, we cannot make the mistake that Absalom did. Although he was deeply disturbed and angered by his sister's incestuous rape, Absalom gave Tamar the impression that she was making a big fuss about nothing.

In 1 Corinthians 5:1-2 God makes it very clear that incest and its continuing results in a victim's life are grave and weighty matters, calling for mourning "in sorrow and in shame."

Verses like these, however, may easily be misinterpreted by the victim of incest. *Sorrow belongs to the victim, but the shame of guilt belongs to the abuser.* Unfortunately, the victim often carries both while the abuser seemingly carries neither.

In most cases the victim is doubly wronged—at the time the actual offense occurs, and every time she relives the shame. She may live with that shame permanently, unable to realize that she does not need to bear the guilt of sin. She has been sinned *against*. *She has been used*.

Hope for healing lies in an understanding of the two personal needs we have discussed earlier. Many incest victims have no sense of security or significance.

A need for emotional security, for a sense of being loved in some way—if only physically—may have prompted the incest victim to submit to her abuser. A need for significance may later motivate her to wield her sexuality as a weapon in family power struggles; she may feel it is the only weapon she has or knows how to use.

Other victims feel condemned to live out their lives in desolation, totally devoid of any form of security or significance.

DEALING WITH THE SHAME OF GUILT

The incest victim who tries to find comfort in the Scriptures may find her sense of guilt intensified by verses like the following when they are taken out of context:

Do you not know that the unrighteous and the wrongdoers will not inherit or have any share in the kingdom of God? Do not be deceived . . . ; neither the impure nor immoral . . . nor adulterers, nor those who participate in homosexuality . . . will inherit or have any share in the kingdom of God. (1 Cor. 6:9-10)

But it's so important to continue reading this passage to find the hope offered there:

And such were some of you (once). *But you were washed clean [purified by a complete atonement for sin and made free from the guilt of sin]; and you were consecrated (set apart, hallowed); and you were justified (pronounced righteous, by trust) in the name of the Lord Jesus Christ and in the (Holy) Spirit of our God.*
Do you not know that your body is the temple—the very sanctuary—of the Holy Spirit Who lives within you, Whom you

have received [as a Gift] from God? You are not your own,
    You were bought for a price—purchased with a preciousness
and paid for, made His own. So then, honor God and bring
glory to Him in your body. (1 Cor. 6:11, 19-20, emphasis mine)

This passage mentions three concepts that are very important to a victim of incest: purification, justification, and consecration. These concepts tie into two of the names of God: Jehovah M'Kaddesh and Jehovah-tsidkenu. Understanding the meanings of these names can free the incest victim from desolation.

An incest victim feels dirty. Purity of body and soul seem unattainable. She feels untouchable. Tainted. Tossed aside.

And Jehovah, as we have seen, is a God of holiness.

An incest victim feels a terrible, crippling guilt. Innocence lies far behind her, buried somewhere back in her early childhood. Now unreachable.

And Jehovah, as we have seen, is a God of righteousness.

An incest victim feels unloved. While other girls are pursuing pleasant fantasies about boys their own age, she feels undesirable. "Spoiled" is the word used in the book *The Color Purple.*

Jehovah is also the God of love.

Oh, really? the incest victim says to herself. *Maybe for normal girls, but not for me.*

HOW CAN THIS HOLY GOD ACCEPT ME?

Jehovah-M'Kaddesh—what a strange-looking name. How on earth do you pronounce it? Its meaning is also elusive: "the God who sanctifies." What does that actually mean? And what part do we play in this process of sanctification? "Consecrate yourselves, therefore, and be holy; for I am the Lord your God. And you shall keep my statutes, and do them. I am the Lord who sanctifies you" (Lev. 20:7-8).

In the Old Testament alone, *sanctify* occurs some seven

hundred times and is often used with the words sanctuary, hallow, and holy. Its primary meaning is *to set apart* or *separate,* as in setting apart holy people, holy places, and remembering the Sabbath "to keep it holy."

But God alone is holy. An old Scottish preacher describes the importance of God's holiness:

It is the balance . . . of all the attributes of Deity. Power without holiness would degenerate into cruelty; omnisicience without holiness would become craft; justice without holiness would degenerate into revenge; and goodness without holiness would be passionate and intemperate fondness doing mischief rather than accomplishing good.

The Old Testament prophet Isaiah became aware of the awesomeness of God's holiness in a vision he received. He saw God sitting on a lofty throne in the temple. Even the heavenly creatures, the seraphim, covered their faces in God's presence while singing: "Holy, holy, holy is the Lord of hosts. . ." (Isa. 6:3).

Isaiah's reaction would be echoed by each one of us, were we placed in those surroundings: "My doom is sealed, for I am a foul-mouthed sinner, a member of a sinful, foul-mouthed race; and I have looked upon the King, the Lord of heaven's armies" (Isa. 6:5, TLB).

But a wonderful thing happened to Isaiah. One of the seraphim flew to the altar and, with a pair of tongs, picked out a burning coal. He touched it to Isaiah's lips and said precious, healing words: "Now you are pronounced 'Not guilty' because this coal has touched your lips. Your sins are all forgiven" (Isa. 6:7, TLB).

Was it the presence of the Lord that had sanctified Isaiah? No, *it was what happened to him when he experienced the presence of this awesomely holy God!* Isaiah had realized his own unholiness, his own impurity, his own sinfulness.

This same man said: "How can such as we be saved? We are all infected and impure with sin. When we put on our prized robes of righteousness we find they are but filthy rags" (Isa. 64:5b-6, TLB).

A literal translation of filthy rags is "menstrual rags." In Isaiah's day, without running water and the level of sanitation we know today, nondisposable menstrual rags were filthy indeed.

Filthy, yes, but washable in a cleansing stream! It is one of God's everyday miracles that blood stains wash out immediately in water.

The burning coal, the cleansing stream—both are symbolic of the supreme Sacrifice whose blood flowed on the cross in that once-for-all Day of Atonement.

Some find it impossible to accept the atonement. They feel they must manufacture their own righteousness. In fact, people have been feeling that way for generations upon generations.

Modern orthodox Jewry still conceives of God as weighing their good deeds over against the bad. On New Year's Day the process begins and on the Day of Atonement it ends and judgment is sealed for the year. The ten days in between are spent in a desperate effort by charity, prayer, and fasting to tip the balances in one's favor, although there is never certainty as to which way it may have gone. [7]

The Hebrew word for righteousness is *tsedek,* originally meaning "to be straight." A righteous person—or one who attempts to become righteous through charity, prayer, fasting, or other good works—is called a *tsadik,* and the righteous God is called *El-Tsadik.*

Jehovah Himself is perfect righteousness, but what can we say about ourselves? David, the Old Testament psalmist, and the apostle Paul concur in their appraisal of our helpless situation: "There is none that doeth good, no not one," David said in Psalm 14:3 (KJV). "There is none righteous, no, not one . . . all have sinned, and come short of the glory of God," echoes Paul (Rom. 3:10, 23, KJV).

A righteous Jehovah cannot overlook a lack of righteousness in any person; he can "by no means clear the guilty" (Num. 14:18). It is impossible for any of us to perfectly obey God's laws, for He sees not only our actions but our thoughts and attitudes.

And so Jehovah became Jehovah-tsidkenu, Jehovah our righteousness.

What we could not do for ourselves, He did for us.

The penalty of death that sin had incurred must be borne by an innocent sufferer, and the innocence of the sufferer must be applied to the sinner. Only on this basis could God declare the guilty to be righteous.

Surely He has borne our griefs—sickness, weakness and distress—and carried our sorrows and pain [of punishment]. . . .

He was wounded for our transgressions, He was bruised for our guilt and iniquities; the chastisement needful to obtain peace and well-being for us was upon Him, and with the stripes that wounded Him we are healed and made whole.

All we like sheep have gone astray, we have turned every one to his own way; and the Lord has made to light on Him the guilt and iniquity of us all.

He shall see the fruit of the travail of His soul and be satisfied; by His knowledge of Himself [which He possesses and imparts to others] shall My [uncompromisingly] righteous One, My Servant, justify and make many righteous—upright and in right standing with God; for He shall bear their iniquities and their guilt [with the consequences, says the Lord]. (Isa. 53:4-6, 11)

The burning coal that cleansed Isaiah's lips and soul acted as an impetus to answer God's burning question: "'Whom shall I send as a messenger to my people? Who will go?' And I said, 'Lord, I'll go! Send me'" (Isa. 6:8, TLB).

May we echo Isaiah's response!

As we confess the sins we have committed *and the sins*

that have been committed against us, Jehovah-tsidkenu reminds us that a once-for-all atonement has been made on the Cross. And Jehovah-M'Kaddesh pleads with us to consecrate wholly what He has made holy and righteous:

I appeal to you . . . and beg of you . . . to make a decisive dedication of your bodies—presenting all your members and faculties—as a living sacrifice, holy (devoted, consecrated) and well pleasing to God, which is your reasonable (rational, intelligent) service and spiritual worship.

Do not be conformed to this world—this age, fashioned after and adapted to its external, superficial customs. But be transformed . . . by the [entire] renewal of your mind—by its new ideals and its new attitude—so that you may prove [for yourselves] what is the good and acceptable and perfect will of. God, even the thing which is good and acceptable and perfect [in His sight for you]. (Rom. 12:1-2)

We have been made acceptable by and in His love. That's security!

We are now accountable to Him for the gifts and ministry He gives each one of us. That's significance!

Those who once were "used" have now become new!

Therefore if any person is (ingrafted) in Christ, the Messiah, he is (a new creature altogether,) a new creation; the old (previous moral and spiritual condition) has passed away. Behold, the fresh and new has come! (2 Cor. 5:17)

WHAT IS THE MEANING OF HIS NAME?
1. The order in which the names of Jehovah appear in the Bible shows purpose and progression in answering the developing spiritual needs of the Hebrew people. Let's review the meanings of the compound names of Jehovah:

Jehovah-jireh. Jehovah provided the ram for Abraham;

previously He had provided a _____ by which Israel was redeemed from Egyptian bondage. The _____ of this Passover offering was applied to the lintels of the Hebrew doorways to signify exemption from the punishment of the death angel (Exod. 12:1-13).

Jehovah-rapha. Jehovah heals life's wounds and makes sweet the waters of Marah, meaning _____. He enables us to develop an attitude of _____ in the midst of problems.

Jehovah-nissi. God's _____ or banner led Joshua against the enemy, _____. That battle is an example or type of the spiritual encounter we face in our Christian lives, as discussed in Ephesians 6:11-18. Which armor is defensive? Which is offensive? What characterizes our enemy? (See 1 John 2:16.)

Jehovah-shalom. Gideon had to face possible persecution or alienation, even from his own _____, in order to find peace.

So we see that Jehovah-jireh provides for our redemption; Jehovah-rapha heals our bitterness toward the past; Jehovah-nissi leads us in battle against our spiritual enemies; Jehovah-shalom teaches that obedience is our source of energy and peace.

This spiritual progression is followed, as we have just seen, by the meaning of Jehovah-M'Kaddesh: the God who sets apart His people in holiness and wholeness. How do we qualify for this special privilege? (See Rom. 12:1-2.) Do our past life or our past experiences disqualify us? (See Rom. 8:10-16; 1 Cor. 6:11.)

2. From the ancient Romans comes the picture of justice as a blindfolded woman holding balanced scales. Read Job's comments on justice in Job 31:6 and David's description of being "weighed in the balances" in Psalm 62:9. In Daniel 5:27, another vivid word picture is given of a life found lacking. With this in mind, reread the quotation on page 166. Think back to a time in the past when you felt

"weighed in the balances and found wanting." Did you try to tip the balances in your favor by doing good deeds? Did you ever feel you had done enough?

3. Although God commanded the Israelites to live righteously, He was well aware that they could not measure up to His standards of righteousness. He also advised them, therefore, to offer the sacrifices of righteousness (Ps. 4:5). What do these sacrifices include? (See Ps. 51:17.)

4. How does God's identity as El-Tsadik make it impossible for Him to overlook the lack of righteousness in people? How has God solved the problem of our unrighteousness? (See 2 Cor. 5:21.)

5. Discuss how the suffering servant of Isaiah 53 is also the Holy One of Isaiah 49:7. The righteousness of the suffering servant is imputed to us as we confess our sins; only His righteousness can balance the scales. Discuss Ephesians 2:9 in this light.

11

Why Is It So Hard for Me to Trust God?

ABBA:
Papa

I wish I had a house like hers
   So big and clean and white.
I wish I had a dad like hers
   To hug and kiss good night.
I wish I had a life like hers
   So happy and so fine.
I wonder if she ever wished
   For anything of mine.

The speaker was talking about children's poetry when the
poem took shape in my mind and seemed to transfer itself
to the paper in front of me. "Poetry for children should
rhyme," she was saying. "Children use a lot of *I*'s when
they talk, so it's OK to use the personal pronoun
frequently. And children's poetry should sound like
something a child, not an adult, would say."

   At the age of thirty-nine, sitting in a group of adults, I
looked at the words I had just written and realized that the

child within me had spoken. The thirty-nine-year-old had experienced certain hang-ups for years because the child within her had gotten "hung up" at a certain point in her maturing.

Somewhere between the ages of ten and twelve my feelings toward my father began to change from a child's accepting love—a fondness that tolerated his moods—to first embarrassment and then resentment.

In the first chapter I mentioned our family's frequent moves, my father's strictness, and his threats of suicide when countermanded. My mother tried to explain to me that Dad's emotional imbalance was probably caused or at least aggravated by the mine explosion in which he was injured and his father killed. However, understanding is not the same as forgiving.

Having recommitted his life to Christ during his convalescence, my father enrolled at a Bible school, hoping to enter the ministry, but his plans were frustrated. So, increasingly, was he. By the time I was born, he had begun to sell encyclopedias and Bibles in what he called "a door-to-door Bible ministry." We lived in a series of trailers and cheaply furnished apartments, usually attending a different church every Sunday. At least in my mind, we were "different" from everyone else. We didn't even have a TV!

The mine explosion, I believe, permanently overshadowed my father's life and made him extremely overprotective of his children. Although he loved me, he seemed deaf, dumb, and blind to *my* interests. I remember snatches of our conversations . . .

"Why do you want to play with those noisy kids? Aren't you Daddy's little girl any more? Come over here and tell me you're Daddy's little girl. I don't want you to play with those children—you might get hurt. Besides, we'll be moving again soon, and you'll forget about them. Just stay home and read a good book."

I remember his saying, "I love you, Joy. I love you in the right way." As a child I never understood that statement.

In sixth grade I began public school for the first time; I had taken the Calvert Correspondence Course up to that point. I was the only girl in the class with long hair, since my father would not allow me to get it cut, and for once his limitations worked to my advantage! I acquired several boyfriends, to my delight—but not to his. Some time that year a boy walked across town with a gift for me; my father answered the door and became terribly upset with me and angry at the boy. In no uncertain terms, he told Danny to leave—and to leave me alone.

From that point on, he repeated a statement many times: "You're too young to think about boys. No dating until you're twenty-one, and don't even think about getting married until you're at least twenty-five!"   Current surveys show that the best marriages do take place when husband and wife are about twenty-five, but I wasn't aware of those statistics at the time!

Whenever I entered a new school—I attended a total of nine—I heard the same old injunctions I had heard as a small child: "Now, I don't want you running around or getting involved in all this school stuff . . ."

No after-school activities, no forensics, no sports—only what I could squeeze into school hours. I wasn't even allowed to be involved in a church youth group or attend a Sunday school class consistently.

Finally, in my senior year, I rebelled and tried out for the senior play. I made the lead part. Practices were after school and I just didn't come home. Dad didn't like it, but he tolerated it.

I knew better, however, than to ask about getting my driver's license. The answer would undoubtedly have been "No!" So, after a little practice, I asked a friend to take me for my test. To my surprise, I passed.

Since I had been assigned to sixth grade after four years of the Calvert Correspondence Course, I was only sixteen during my senior year of high school. My embarrassment over our life-style and my constant feelings of being "left

out" had turned to anger and resentment toward my
father. I repressed most of my rebellion, knowing all too
well the effects of my father's anger.

But now all my friends were applying to colleges. As
valedictorian of my class, I had opportunities for
scholarships at several colleges. When I tried to discuss the
subject with Dad, the conversation went something like
this: "We don't have to make this decision yet." (This was
spring of my senior year.) "I'll decide what we're going to
do in August. If you go, we'll move closer to the college
and I'll take you back and forth to classes every day . . .
Joy, I wish you were still Daddy's little girl. You don't act
like you love your daddy any more."

I realized that my parents had paid for my brother's
college and seminary and that there was no money left
over to finance my education. I didn't resent my brother; I
knew that, as a child and teenager, he had received
beatings (with a belt) that he did not deserve, just for
reacting like a normal child. I lived in constant fear of
arousing my father's anger—and the results of that anger.

Is it any wonder that I was confused as to what "love"
meant?

And is it any wonder that my concept of a heavenly
Father centered around the Old Testament statement: "I the
Lord your God am a *jealous* God" (Deut. 4:9)?

To me that meant more of the same—an overprotective,
smothering father figure who cared little or nothing about
my abilities or goals.

Several days after my high school graduation, I left
home, acting on the counsel of my English teacher and my
high school principal who were both very concerned about
my getting an education. This enabled the judge of the
juvenile court to intercede with my father on my behalf.
The court proceedings, although held privately, deeply hurt
and humiliated my parents, which I have always regretted.
Finally, however, my father reluctantly agreed to let me
become a boarding student at Messiah College, where I

had been offered a scholarship. I worked and borrowed my way to a B.A. degree.

When I left home, I left behind separate letters for my mother and father. I could not confide in my mother ahead of time because I did not want her to be blamed for my actions.

I did not, however, leave behind my resentment toward my father.

Although I rejected him emotionally and transferred my affections to others (at the age of seventeen, to my future husband), the empty spot in my life began to cause problems. I found myself developing "crushes" on older men. Most of these I dismissed as normal (Doesn't everyone have crushes on good-looking teachers?), and most of the feelings disappeared during courtship and the early years of marriage.

A strange dream involving a minister whom I loved and respected, however, became a source of guilt. I feared that the dream showed repressed sexual urges and wondered what was wrong with me, since the minister was old enough to be my father.

I simply did not realize my growing need for communication with and reassurance from a father figure.

During the years when our children were born, I struggled with envy toward other women who had a good relationship with their fathers and whose children were able to spend quality time with "Grandpa." I wrestled with "it's-just-not-fair" feelings in my attitudes toward these women, but still wasn't sure *why* I felt the way I did. Was it competition? Inferiority? Just plain jealousy?

To complicate matters, my negative feelings were not limited to my father alone; the pattern repeated itself in other relationships. Embarrassment served to detonate the inner timebomb of my emotions; when something in my relationships with other people caused me to feel embarrassment, I became upset. Later, my husband's sense of humor would often touch a sore spot and the fuse would ignite. I would be terribly hurt, embarrassed, or angered by what my husband (and later my sons) described as "just a joke!"

As I look back on my relationship with my father, I see the greatest barriers between us as his anger and his unrealistic, ever-present expectations of me. At times I still struggle with a feeling of "never quite measuring up" to God's expectations of me, and I fear reprisal when I make mistakes or wrong decisions.

When these struggles occur I lean strongly on promises my heavenly Father has given me:

For I know the thoughts and plans that I have for you, says the Lord, thoughts and plans for welfare and peace, and not for evil, to give you hope in your final outcome. . . . Yes, I have loved you with an everlasting love; therefore with loving-kindness have I drawn you and have continued My faithfulness to you. (Jer. 29:11; 31:3)

A FATHER'S ANGER

But an earthly father's anger creates deep wounds, wounds that leave lasting scars. I think of my friend Samantha, who as an older student has been an inspiration to everyone around her by going back to college and earning her B.A. degree. Samantha also still struggles with her "father image." She explained her emotional and spiritual dilemma to me several years ago.

Dear Joy,
It all started with a phone call from Mom. It was a regular call until just before she hung up, when she stated rather matter-of-factly: "Your father has been beating on your sister again. She has a lot of chest pain and she has been coughing up blood."

Then Mom went on and asked me how work was going.

After she hung up, I sat in the office with my mind whirling in familiar old circles. How can he do that? How can beat on his own daughter?

Theoretically speaking, I could understand ("explain") my father. Along with a head injury, mid-life crisis had caused him to have many psychological problems. These complicated his physical problems.

How can you love and hate someone at the same time? This is how I felt. The logical part of me said, "He can't help it." But with the other part of me I wanted to beat on him myself.

When I went back to my apartment, my roommates must have noticed I had been crying. One of them asked what was wrong. How can you tell someone your father beats your sister? I felt so ashamed, but I knew I had to talk or I'd explode. Of course, she had no answers.

The next day I took time off work to go to my family. Why? Was I thinking I could put a Band-Aid on a giant ulcer and make it go away? Did I have any answers? Would my presence give them all a desire to change their ways? Why was I going home? I didn't really know. I just had to go.

So why had I driven for hours to come home? I guess because I just had to find out how things were.

My dad professes to be a Christian. So why does he act like this? Is he really going to end up in hell? How can I help him? He has gone to mental health clinics for years—all they do is medicate him. They can't seem to counsel well enough to help him change his behavior.

How can I love him? How can I not be afraid of him? I force myself to do things for him, hoping the act will eventually produce some type of positive feelings for him. After all, the Bible doesn't say to do good to others only if you feel like it. It says to praise God whether you feel like it or not. So why doesn't love come? Will it always be just an act? And what does God think of my attitude toward my earthly father? And where are the answers to all these questions?

Samantha

Over the years I have come to understand that all too often, negative emotions toward an earthly father prevent a positive, mature relationship with a heavenly Father. In his book entitled *Healing of Memories,* Dr. David Seamands includes a fascinating chart: "How the Good News Becomes the Bad News." Studying the chart helped me recognize the following dilemmas:

If my earthly father is mean and unforgiving, it is difficult to think of my heavenly Father as good and merciful.

If my earthly father is unpredictable and untrustworthy, can the heavenly Father be steadfast and reliable?

If my earthly father is absent when I need him, how can a heavenly Father be ever-present and available?

If my earthly father is a killjoy, why should a heavenly Father be a giver of good gifts?

If my earthly father is unjust and unfair, is anyone holy, just, and impartial?

If my earthly father is critical and difficult to please, how do I trust God to be nurturing and affirming?

If my earthly father rejects me, will my heavenly Father accept me?

It is only after we have disentangled our "heavenly Father image" from our "earthly father image" that we can relinquish feelings of resentment toward the God who permitted our family situations. It becomes much easier to release a fellow human from our expectations of him or her when we have learned to put our faith only in God (Ps. 62:5). We can recognize that any and all humans will fail us—especially when many times those same humans have been hurt by their own parents and are unable to break the cycle.

Even after we have recognized our confusion, however, the healing process will probably take time. And remember—understanding is not the same as forgiving.

Samantha's questions were familiar to me: "How can I love my father? Why doesn't love come? Will it always be just an act? And what does God think of my attitude toward my earthly father?"

I vividly remember standing in the foyer of my home

church years ago and asking our dearly beloved pastor, the
Reverend Fred Fowler, those very questions.

I had asked my father for forgiveness and had received it.
I no longer felt resentment, but neither could I seem to feel
the love I wanted to feel. And I felt like a hypocrite.

Pastor Fowler smiled at me in his loving, fatherly way
and said, "Just do the things you would do if you felt love
toward your father. Don't wait for the emotion to come;
just continue doing right things and God will reward you."

I did . . . and He did. In His time.

I learned that when emotions seem totally dead, love
becomes an act of the will.

A FATHER'S ABSENCE

I ran away from my father's anger and his expectations.
During the years that I was growing increasingly resentful
toward my father, a cousin of mine was also experiencing a
deep hurt in a very different way—a father's absence. I'll
let Pat tell you about it herself from one of her letters.

*My earthly father died when I was fairly young—twelve years of
age. Although my father's health had been impaired due to an
earlier condition, his death was sudden. It was such a traumatic
experience that only recently was I able to understand how it
affected me at the time.*

*I'm sure most children take their parents for granted and
expect them to be there forever. I was no exception. Upon my
father's death I grieved tremendously. It seemed as though
everywhere I looked was evidence of his having lived. Every room
of the house and everything in view in our yard brought
crushing memories. The memories were alive and yet Dad was
dead.*

*I carried most of my grief with me silently. My mother was
overburdened with her sense of loss. Many times, late at night, I
would awaken to hear her sobbing and I would try to comfort
her. At school I became somewhat withdrawn. I knew of only*

*one other student whose parent had died. And divorce was not
nearly as common then. I felt very inferior.*

*Sometimes, unknowingly, small children can be so cruel. A
child, without thinking, had informed me: "I don't like you any
more—your father died."*

*Her remark had a lasting effect on me. I guarded against
letting people know that my father was dead. I especially
remember a time in school when a teacher asked each student in
the class to name his or her father's occupation. I dreaded
answering the question so much that I almost became physically
sick. I shrank down in my seat as the teacher moved up and
down the aisles. To my great relief, he stopped before he got to my
desk.*

*Unfortunately, I truly did believe I was an outcast. The pain
was intense, but all the while I was trying not to let it show.*

*Looking back, I can see how these and many other incidents
deeply affected my behavior. It's sad that no one close to me
understood. A few sincere talks with an understanding
individual would have helped ease my pain. Perhaps people
tried, but I was too locked into my situation to notice.*

*I was extremely fortunate, though. I had fond memories of my
dad teaching Sunday school classes and leading the church in
prayer as he knelt by his pew. My Christian upbringing enabled
me to reach out and accept my heavenly Father's love. Praise
God for His care, for His Scriptures, and for the love He showed
me through His Son Jesus. People might fail us but He never
does.*

*God has been healing me of those early hurts in very unique
and special ways. My mother remarried, and her second
husband was a loving and generous man. God has given me
opportunities and insights to reach out to others in His name.*

*Having recently attended a women's retreat where you spoke,
I reflected on many things. You referred to many women of the
Bible; it was so evident across the hundreds, even thousands, of
years how much modern-day women do have in common with
them. Isn't it fascinating how God can minister to all our needs,
in our similarities and in our differences?*

My heavenly Father has been a real treasure to me—perhaps I've felt His presence closer than other women as a result of my father's death.

Someone has said that difficult experiences in life make us either bitter or better. Pat obviously holds no bitterness against God for taking her father; her life has been filled with a caring stepfather, a loving husband, and the laughter of children. Other women have not recovered as well or as quickly as Pat did.

A FATHER'S ABUSE

During a women's retreat I felt led to talk about the resentment I had experienced toward my father. One of the listeners interpreted my words to mean that I had experienced sexual abuse from my father, as she had. Although our backgrounds were dissimilar, my words helped her to face her own past, as she wrote to me later— a past filled with abuse.

If you had not shared your bitterness toward your dad, I wouldn't be free from the same bitterness and resentment toward my dad. I've been carrying it around and didn't realize he was involved. I've been confessing and asking for forgiveness pertaining to other things and other people, but Dad has been the root of all of it. I was molested, dominated, put down by him for many years.

I longed for Jesus to be Lord of my life—in my heart and life, not just in my head—to be able to trust Him completely, in and with everything. There was a blockage there and I didn't know what it was. Perhaps I should add here that I have been going to a counseling center for nine months. By the Lord's grace and help I feel I've made tremendous progress, as last July I was really on the bottom . . . thinking about suicide, the whole bit. Anyway, we got over or through many barriers, but this one with my dad was buried so deep it wouldn't surface. (At least I wouldn't let it—why should I? He was dead; what did it matter?)

Praise God, my eyes were opened and it's all forgiven! I feel pounds lighter! There is nothing between me and my Savior tonight!

I might clarify one thing—Dad gave his heart to the Lord a year before he died. . . .

The author of the letter has become my friend and correspondent. A paramedic who is regularly exposed to the realities of sexual abuse, she has helped to found a group called Sex Abuse Survivors and has gone back to school to work toward a degree. In the meantime she is also working actively with children's services. My friend is a healed helper.

A FATHER'S APATHY

There is one more letter I would like to share with you, a letter I was handed at a retreat. I have not been able to track down the writer. The letter deals with a father's apathy.

Dear Joy,

I'm writing to you because I know that I could not express verbally all that God has done for me without sobbing for hours.

He has truly healed me in the area of father-daughter relationships!

I was the fourth child to my parents and was Daddy's little girl. He took me everywhere, and my life revolved around his attention. My parents owned a home business so we were virtually always together.

When I was seven, my parents—then forty-two and forty-four—had a baby boy. I was instantly dethroned and my baby brother became everyone's all-in-all. I can specifically trace my compulsive overeating to that age; of course, I was attempting to get that warmth from food.

My dad was an alcoholic, and his drinking progressed steadily. It became a problem to me when I hit my teens. I began to seek male attention, always with the wrong kind of boy. I constantly sought out the boys with problems. Of course I thought I would cure them—and usually did—and when they got it together, I would move on to my next hopeless case and further upset my family.

I eventually went into nursing. Again, I hoped to cure the world. At the age of twenty, I became pregnant by a boy that I had dated for ten months and was engaged to. He went off the deep end—he could not face his affluent family with the news— and turned to drugs. I thank God because a marriage to him would have been disastrous.

I can remember so vividly being in a Salvation Army home for unwed mothers. After my family would visit, I cried for days because my dad seemed to age ten years with each visit. One day in counseling I cried out, "I have hurt my father so much. How will he ever forgive me?" The counselor said, "More to the point, dear child, will you forgive your father for the way he has hurt you?"

From that point on I began to realize how rejection from my father had affected my life.

I gave my daughter up for adoption and desperately tried to start my life off in a new, positive direction.

After much counseling, I finally chose a wonderful man to marry, but when I accepted the Lord into my life, the problems really began. I could not understand "the Father's love." I could not accept God as my Father—as my God, but not as my Father. I saw pastors and Christian psychologists for help, but to no avail. I remember saying to one, "If God had given her *only begotten son to shed His blood for my sins, I could understand the sacrifice—a mother's love is real—but His only begotten son does not touch my heart." A father's love was not real to me.*

A year ago, I saw my new pastor for more counseling on this ever-present problem. I told him that I had heard a woman, in praise and worship, say, "I love You, Father," and I knew that I must get to the root problem in my life, that I must be free to love

*God as my Father. I talked to him for weeks. In one session he
asked me if my dad—who, by the way, had been deceased for
twelve years—had been sitting in the office with us and had
been asked if I were a blessing in his life or a heartache, what
would be say? I said, "A blessing." I was probably thinking of
the first seven years of my life. Well, the pastor prayed that the
Holy Spirit would reveal to me the true relationship that we had,
that I would see the real truth of my dad's love for me.*

*I went home emotionally drained and soon developed a
migraine. When I awoke at midnight, I went to my dining
room, away from my sleeping family, and poured my heart out
to God, asking for the truth to be revealed. I said: "Lord, if I've
been lied to, cheated of my dad's love by one who comes to steal,
rob, and destroy, then show me—and restore all that the locusts
have eaten away."*

*A miracle took place for the next four hours. God gave me
visions and memories of my dad, times that I had blocked from
my mind and replaced with negative memories. Sure, there were
bad times, but I had allowed Satan to cheat me and steal from
me all the good memories until only the bad became reality to
me.*

*I can't express the times God through His Holy Spirit restored
to me. For hours and hours every wonderful moment of closeness
came back, and I began to see all the hard times as just a
consequence of my dad's alcoholism. God gave me the ability to
detach those times from my dad and to call sin "sin," but it no
longer diminished my dad's love for me.*

*I remembered how we would walk on the farm together—or
work in the store together, how he would ask me for a backrub
when I was in nurses' training and rave about them. I
remembered the tears in his eyes as he walked me down the aisle
on my wedding day—and, at the end of his life, how he slipped
into a coma, only minutes after I had driven four hours to see
him.*

*In the final analysis I knew that I was still Daddy's little girl,
and he had never stopped loving me. Because he didn't know
Jesus he was unable to push the alcohol behind him and go on
giving that love to his family as God intended. I can only feel*

sympathy for my dad's life, and I thank God I can break the cycle *because I have Jesus.*

So now I'm able to love my "Abba Father" and, most of all, receive from Him a perfect Father's love.

In His love,
Kathy

Perhaps you felt mixed emotions as you read these letters. Perhaps you too may not be able to say the word "father" without experiencing a hollow feeling in the pit of your stomach, or even nausea.

Perhaps for years you have confused the actions of an earthly father (or grandfather or brother or uncle) with the intentions of your heavenly Father.

It might help you to use the name Jesus used when speaking to His Father: "Abba." For those of us who have been adopted into the family of God through accepting Jesus Christ as Savior, "God has sent the (Holy) Spirit of His Son into our hearts, crying, Abba (Father)! Father!" (Gal.4:6).

Some years ago I heard bright-eyed little Israeli children calling "Abba!" in tones of affection and trust. The word is simply a baby word for Papa, a word that can be pronounced without any teeth. It is a word of complete abandonment, a word used in the beginning of a new life.

As God the Father—"Abba"—welcomes you into His family and forgives your sins upon confession, so He will give you the ability to forgive those who have sinned against you. Perhaps they too have been sinned against. In any case, forgiving will release you from the bondage of hatred, and the past can be put behind you.

Abba's children can trust Him.

WHAT IS THE MEANING OF HIS NAME?

1. "Abba" is the common Aramaic word used by a Hebrew child to address its father. The Lord's Prayer is significant in that not only did Jesus use the word "Father," but He

authorized others to use it as well. Who were—and are—these others? Does the meaning of this name permeate your prayer life? (See Gal. 4:6.)

2. Jeremias, the great German New Testament scholar, says that Jesus used the word "Abba" in all His prayers except for His cry in Matthew 27:46—"My God, My God, why hast thou forsaken Me?" (KJV), where He quoted Psalm 22:1. What was His final prayer on the cross? (See Luke 23:46.)

3. The Hebrews of Jesus' day were so intent on guarding the sovereignty and transcendence of God that they never repeated His covenant name, Yahweh. Instead, they invented the name Jehovah, made of a combination of two separate names of God. How were the prayers of Jesus revolutionary in the way they addressed God?

4. One of the works of the Holy Spirit is to help Christians understand the meaning of their relationship with El-Tsadik, the righteous God who is also their Abba. How does this understanding change our spirit? (See Rom. 8:15-17.)

5. Kent Hughes, in his book *Abba Father,* points out three benefits of a Father-child understanding:
    a. A sense of being loved
    b. The reality of forgiveness
    c. Confidence and security
    Pinpoint any problem area in your life . . . and ask Abba about it.

6. Kent Hughes has called the possessive pronoun used in Jesus' address of God—"*our* Father"—the "pronoun of partnership." Hughes also says that "the Fatherhood of God enriches life vertically and horizontally."[1] In what ways is this true in your life?

7. In the Lord's Prayer, the phrase "who art in Heaven" emphasizes the sovereignty of our divine "Abba." Do you think it is possible to become flippant or oversentimental

about our relationship with our heavenly Father? If so, how can we guard against it?

8. How do we keep echoes of past parental relationships from interfering with our present relationship with "Abba Father"? Why is anger, absence, apathy, or abuse from an earthly father hurtful to a child's spiritual as well as emotional growth? Have you been aware of any negative transfer from your relationship with an earthly father to your relationship with "Abba Father"? What determines whether life's difficult experiences make us "bitter or better"? Discuss Hebrews 12:15.

9. In Psalm 62:5 we are cautioned to put our trust only in God. What often happens, however, when we are disappointed by human representatives of God? Why is understanding not the same as forgiving?

10. Perhaps as you read this chapter, you yearned for the fullness of a Father-child relationship with God. It can be experienced only by accepting salvation through Jesus Christ, who was sent by our Father to satisfy the demands of justice. Pray the following prayer to accept this gift: "I realize that I am a sinner. I realize I can't save myself. I repent—I turn my back to sin. Thank you, Jesus, for taking the punishment for my sin. Thank you, Abba Father, for accepting your Son as a substitute sin-bearer. I believe in your power to erase the effects of the past, and I invite you to create new life within me."

12

Where Was God When I Needed Him?

ABBA:
My heavenly Father

There is no ongoing spiritual life without the process of letting go. At the precise point where we refuse, growth stops. If we hold tightly to anything given to us, unwilling to let it go when the time comes to let it go, or unwilling to allow it to be used as the Giver means it to be used, we stunt the growth of the soul.[1]

Of all the cards and letters I received during my mother's terminal illness—and I appreciated all of them—the following letter meant the most.

Dear Joy,
I just wanted to share something I heard on Sunday in our lesson on Job: "Faith Wrestles with Suffering." Our teacher said, "Faith is when I am left with shattered plans and know He has better plans."

I know so many Scriptures I have given others, but I must read them to myself now. It is so hard to understand why the Lord would take your mother and my dear friend home at this time. They are so needed by so many people. He could have healed them instantly.

"Thou will keep him in perfect peace, whose mind is stayed on thee." They are singing that on the radio just now. He is our peace. They just quoted Philippians 4:6-9 . . . but nothing seems to help me and probably you right now.

I must get to bed before it's morning and time to get up. Now they are singing the song "When I think I'm going under, part the waters, Lord. Touch my life, still the raging storm in me. When I cry for help, oh, hear me, Lord, and hold out Your hand."

It is so good He holds my hand, for I can't seem to hold on lately.

I'll keep praying for you and me, though. He won't fail.

In His love,
Rose

Some people would call this letter negative; probably the writer herself felt she had failed to comfort me. But she *did* comfort me, in a most meaningful way, because *I knew she understood how I felt.*

THE FACTS OF FAITH

About a month after Mother's death I wrote the following reflection.

"Mother, please talk to me!" I pleaded silently. *"Talk about Heaven. Tell me that you're anxious to see Jesus . . ."*

Mixed feelings struggled within me as I sat by my mother's bedside. All my life I had listened to her vibrant testimony of her salvation, of her glowing faith in Jesus Christ, and of her heart's desire to see Him face to face.

Now, as her life ebbed into the distant horizon, I had somehow expected to see angels—or at least hear about them from her.

But a nine-year bout with cancer, cobalt, and finally

chemotherapy had reduced Mother's energy level to a pathetic low. With scarcely enough strength to cope with the physical realities one day at a time, there was little energy for looking ahead, even to spiritual realities.

Her motto had been "Keep looking up!" but now pain and nausea clouded her outlook and her uplook. For the past year, during her residence at the Alliance Home, Mother had delighted in telling our family story after story about her friends and their activities there. Now, in comparison, she seemed strangely quiet.

I tried to sing the hymns Mother had always loved, but my voice broke on the first few phrases of "Jesus Is the Sweetest Name I Know." Mother didn't seem to notice; she had fallen asleep. Psalm 91 had always been her favorite; now the familiar words—"I will deliver (her) and honor (her)," Mother's paraphrase—stuck in my throat during bedside readings. When I stopped reading, she would make no comment. The words seemed meaningless to her, as did my presence.

I felt like a bewildered child. I was slowly losing my mother; was I losing the heritage of her faith as well?

Weeks went by before I began to realize what God was saying in the silence. Although I had trusted Jesus as my Savior and Lord years earlier, to some extent I was depending on my mother's faith. When it seemed to lose its vibrancy, I experienced traumatic doubts about the reality of heaven and all she had taught me.

For thirty-eight years, consciously or unconsciously, I had reassured myself: "The Bible must be true; Mother believes every word. Prayer really must work, because I know it's what has sustained her through all these years. Heaven must be real, because she's looking forward to it so intensely."

Somehow I had missed the meaning of Hebrews 11:1, a familiar passage I had memorized years earlier. A midweek Bible study prompted me to read it in The Amplified Bible:

Now faith is the assurance (the confirmation, the title-deed) of the things [we] hope for, being the proof of things [we] do not see and the conviction of their reality—faith perceiving as real fact what is not revealed to the senses." (Emphasis mine)

Perhaps I had hoped to hear God's voice break the silence. There was no sonic boom, but a meaningful note came to Mother from a friend: "This crucible of misery will soon be past—and you shall see Jesus face to face. Someday we shall worship Him together. You so well know that He loves you. . . ."

If I had hoped to catch a glimpse of angels fluttering beside her bedside, none were visible to me. But as Mother thanked the nurses, on the last night of her life, for their loving care, one of them remarked: "She's an angel. Has she always been this grateful?"

I may not have felt tangible support from above, but I felt God's touch through childish arms that hugged me and youthful voices that spoke words of wisdom: "It's OK, Mom. Remember, she always told us not to be sad at her funeral because she'll be so happy!"

I had been looking for reassurance in things I could sense and feel, in the person who had always been there to comfort me. Now my heavenly Father was teaching me to look to Him in a new way, to perceive "as real fact" what was "not revealed to the senses."

Thanks to the intuitive caring of sensitive staff members at the Alliance Home, I was privileged to spend most of Mother's last night on earth with her. About five in the morning, when she smiled at me and told me to go home and get some rest, I obeyed. Three hours later, she sighed and murmured "Oh Lord, oh Lord!" as she was ushered into His presence.

Oh, Lord . . . even when we feel least conscious of Your power and strength, You are Lord—and faith is fact!

FEELING LIKE A SPIRITUAL FAILURE

During those tearing, terrible, therapy-filled last four months of my mother's life, I felt like a spiritual failure. I couldn't see God working. I couldn't hear Him speak. His presence seemed elusive.

Now, however, I recognize His faithfulness.

More than twenty years earlier God gave me a friend in the form of a sister-in-law, a friend who understands my reactions when I don't understand them myself. During my mother's illness Ramona seemed to sense my need to hear Mother express her faith, even though Mother was too weak and ill to speak. Ramona spent time talking to Mother, expressing the words I couldn't speak but wanted to say and needed to hear.

Other dear friends visited Mother with me or on days when I couldn't get to the hospital or nursing home. Their support was invaluable to me.

Notes and cards were also a real uplift during this time, lending a sense of purpose to an otherwise unexplainable suffering. I realized what a blessing my mother's life had been to so many people.

And my husband and sons—what a joy they were to her and to me! My sons would make a party out of our visits, wheeling Mother all over the Home, making everyone laugh who saw us. Like the day we tried a wig on Mother's balding head and took her for a trial run for the Easter parade!

During those last four months, even our eight-year-old would sit for long periods of time and lovingly stroke Mother's cheek and arm. Amazingly to me, he handled our visits much better than I did. His faith never faltered.

But I emphasize again, for the sake of others who may also feel like their spiritual lives failed in the face of grief, *mine did*! I went through stages of terrible anxiety, anger, resentment, even rage at the lack of justice in this awful world. What had my sweet, gentle mother ever done to deserve this? The answer was obvious: *Nothing.*

HEAD KNOWLEDGE TO HEART KNOWLEDGE

I imagine Martha experienced this same range of emotions—from anxiety to rage—as she waited for Jesus to come to Bethany. She had sent him word that her only brother, Lazarus, was ill.

"Surely He will come at once and heal my brother!" she probably said the first day, in anticipation.

"Perhaps the message has not reached Him . . . perhaps He has to complete another task. . . ." The second day was torn with anxiety and a bit of anger.

On the third day Martha may have cried incredulously, resentfully: "Is it possible that the Master does not care?"

"I cannot imagine He would put us through this agony!" I can hear her protest as they prepared Lazarus for the tomb on the fourth day.

And then Martha learned that Jesus was on His way, and she went out to meet Him, to confront Him with her burning question: "Master, if You had been here, my brother would not have died" (John 11:21).

Don't you think she was asking in her heart:

Where were You when we needed You?
  How could you let us down?
We waited for Your coming despite reproving frowns.
He waited for You too, my Lord, although he could not speak
When all his strength had disappeared
  and fever reached its peak.

He wouldn't have died if You had come,
  come when we sent for You.
We gave You time to get here, Lord—an extra day or two.
We know this area's dangerous, but how Your heart must bleed!
Why didn't You come and save His life? O Lord,
  You knew our need![2]

With extraordinary presence of mind Martha added: "And even now *I know* that whatever You ask from God He will grant it to You" (John 10:22, italics mine). For all the put-downs she has endured through the centuries, Martha's comments show that this "housewife" was a thinker! Perhaps her life had changed since the incident mentioned in Luke 10:38-42.

Jesus' first recorded words must have seemed rather detached, with a curious lack of empathy or sympathy: "Your brother shall rise again" (John 11:23).

Martha's reply was immediate and knowledgeable: *"I know* that he will rise again at the resurrection in the last day" (John 11:24, italics mine).

Jesus' next statement would have been startling to anyone who had not listened carefully over the past three years. Perhaps Martha, along with her sister Mary, had begun to listen to Jesus after His loving rebuke in Luke 10:41: "Martha, Martha, you are anxious and troubled about many things; there is need of but a few things, or only one."

But back to the present. Jesus is saying something radically important:

I am [Myself] the Resurrection and the Life. Whoever believes in—adheres to, trusts in and relies on—Me, although he may die, yet he shall live. And whoever continues to live and believes . . . on Me shall never [actually] die at all. Do you believe this? (John 11:25-26)

Martha, do you believe this? Joy, do you believe this?

Yes, Lord, I have believed—I do believe—that You are the Messiah, the Anointed One, the Son of God, [even He] Who was to come into the world. [It is for Your coming that the world has waited.] (John 11:27)

Notice Martha's replies: "I know, I know—I have believed."

Martha believed in the power at Jesus' disposal. She

believed that if He had been present, He could have healed
Lazarus. She believed that Jesus had a special intimacy
with God and that whatever Jesus asked, God would do.

Martha had a faultless program of belief. She had a
sound "head knowledge." But Jesus wanted her head
knowledge to become heart knowledge.

Oswald Chambers, the beloved author of *My Utmost for
His Highest,* draws a personal application from Martha's
story.

*Is there something like that in the Lord's dealing with you? Is
Jesus educating you into a personal intimacy with Himself? Let
Him press home His question to you—"Believest thou this?"
What is your ordeal of doubt? Have you come, like Martha, to
some overwhelming passage in your circumstances where your
program of belief is about to emerge into a personal belief? This
can never be until a personal need arises out of a personal
problem.*

*To believe is to commit. In the program of mental belief I
commit myself and abandon all that is not related to that
commitment. In personal belief I commit myself morally to this
way of confidence and refuse to compromise with any other; and
in particular belief I commit myself spiritually to Jesus Christ,
and determine in that thing to be dominated by the Lord alone.*

*When I stand face to face with Jesus Christ and He says to
me—"Believest thou this?" I find that faith is as natural as
breathing, and I am staggered that I was so stupid as not to trust
Him before.* [3]

But Martha was still struggling. The certainty of death
was all too real in her mind and recent in her memory.
What was the Master trying to tell her?

It was too much to handle all at once. It was easier to
keep busy. Martha headed for home to tell Mary that Jesus
had come.

Notice how differently the sisters handled their grief.
Martha had to keep moving. Perhaps she had initially

heard from the servants, while doing the housework, that Jesus was in the area. But Mary was immobilized, caught in the paralysis of grief.

When she heard this she sprang up quickly and went to Him. . . . When Mary came to the place where Jesus was and saw Him, she dropped down at His feet, saying to Him, Lord, if you had been here my brother would not have died. (John 11:29, 32)

Notice that Mary's words are almost an exact repetition of Martha's. But her posture was different. She fell down at His feet.

Her body language was saying, "I don't understand why, Lord, but I know You are in control. You are Master. You are Lord."

When Jesus saw her sobbing, and the Jews who came with her [also] sobbing, He was deeply moved in spirit and troubled—He chafed in spirit, and sighed and was disturbed. And He said, Where have you laid him? They said to Him, Lord, come and see. Jesus wept. (John 11:33-35)

On one hand Jesus' reaction was like that of a powerful stallion, full of energy and strength, chafing because that awesome power was being held back. Yet this extraordinary power was balanced by the tenderness of tears.

If the sisters had doubted that Jesus *cared*, their doubts were dispelled by those tears.

Now Jesus, again sighing repeatedly and deeply disquieted, approached the tomb. It was a cave—a hole in the rock—and a boulder lay against [the entrance to close] it. Jesus said, Take away the stone. Martha, the sister of the dead man, exclaimed, But Lord, by this time he [is decaying and] throws off an offensive odor, for he has been dead four days! (John 11:38-39)

"But Lord!"

There were still doubts about Jesus' power. The boulder was symbolic of those doubts. It did not block His power; it simply kept the onlookers from seeing the results of His power.

Jesus said to her, Did I not tell you and promise you that if you would believe and rely on Me, you should see the glory of God?

So they took away the stone. And Jesus lifted up His eyes and said, Father, I thank You that You have heard Me.

Yes, I know that You always hear and listen to Me; but I have said this on account of and for the benefit of the people standing around, so that they may believe You did send Me. . . .

When He had said this, He shouted with a loud voice, Lazarus, come out!

And out walked the man who had been dead, his hands and feet wrapped in burial cloths (linen strips), and with a [burial] napkin bound around his face. Jesus said to them, Free him of the burial wrappings and let him go. (John 11:40-44)

"Free him . . . let him go!"

Lazarus was not the only person who was "let go," who was freed that day. I feel sure that his sisters, Martha and Mary, were freed as well. Freed from doubt. Freed from fear. Freed from programs of belief, anchored merely in the mind.

Freed to heart-trust a heavenly Father. Freed to rely on His Son. Freed to believe that this powerful God cared tenderly for each one of them.

For Jesus had prayed to His Father: "Abba, Father. . . ." In Mary and Martha's day this was a radical, revolutionary concept. God, the holy and righteous Jehovah, was Jesus' Father!

And not only Jesus' Father!

Dr. J. I. Packer said:

The revelation to the believer that God is his Father is in a sense the climax of the Bible, just as it was a final step in the revelatory process which the Bible records. In Old Testament times, as we have seen, God gave His people a covenant name by which to speak of Him and call upon Him: the name Yahweh . . . the great "I am."

But in the New Testament we find that things have changed . . . something has been added. A new factor has come in. New Testament believers deal with God as their Father. "Father" is the name by which they call Him. "Father" has now become His covenant name—for the covenant which binds Him to His people now stands revealed as a family covenant. Christians are His children, His own sons and heirs. And the stress of the New Testament is not on the difficulty and danger of drawing near to the holy God, but on the boldness and confidence with which believers may approach Him: a boldness which springs directly from faith in Christ, and from the knowledge of His saving work.

You sum up the whole of New Testament teaching in a single phrase, if you speak of it as a revelation of the fatherhood of the holy Creator.[4]

Jesus' prayer can be ours: "Father, I thank You that You have heard Me."

In a more contemporary way, singer Christine Wyrtzen expresses the fulfillment of this built-in yearning for a relationship and reunion with our heavenly Father:

I've longed for this place,
And now I'm standing inside.
I can't believe this moment is finally here.
My senses drink it in.
Am I dreaming again?
If I close my eyes,
Will all of this disappear?

I'm in my Father's home.
He's been waiting here for me.

I can tell by the way I feel at home.
I'm in my Father's home.
Here's everything I need.
Words can't describe the feelings in this home.

Soon I'll stand in His presence,
On the grounds of His grace.
Seeing my dream coming true.
I've waited so long
Just to look in His face
Do I hear my name?
I turn to look.
Is it You?

It is my Lord, my Friend,
It seems I've known You all my life.
Oh, what a love I feel your eyes pour into mine!
And as I run to You
You come toward me with open arms.
Here is everything I've hoped all my life to find!

I'm in my Father's home,
He's been waiting here for me.
I can tell by the way He called my name.
I'm in my Father's home,
Here is everything I need.
Words can't describe the feelings in this home.
I've been longing for this day.
Now with loved ones I can say,
Forever we're together in His home!
We're in our Father's home![5]

WHAT IS THE MEANING OF HIS NAME?

1. What is the difference between head knowledge and heart knowledge of God? Many times the transition from one to the other takes place in times of crisis. Can you give any examples from your own life?

2. How did grief affect Mary and Martha differently? How do *you* react to grief? How do you work through it? Do you allow enough time?

3. What simple human reaction proved to the sisters and those around them that Jesus cared about their grief? (See John 11:35.) What does this tell us about the expression of grief?

4. What symbolism do you find in the boulder in front of Lazarus' burial cave? Are there any boulders blocking your faith in Christ's power?

5. By using the address "Abba Father" in His prayer, Jesus was publicly proclaiming His Sonship and hence His divinity. What danger did this entail? (See John 11:53.) Where did Jesus go to prepare for what would come next? (See John 11:54.)

6. How is God's New Testament name different from His Old Testament names? How does God verify His Fatherhood to us? (See Rom. 8:16.)

7. God's fatherly relationship to Jesus involved four factors: authority (John 4:34; 5:19; 6:38; 17:4); affection (John 5:20; 15:9); fellowship (John 8:29; 16:32); honor (John 5:22; 17:1).[6] Since God is our Father as well, we can also experience each of these elements in our relationship with Him. Of the four areas above, which is the strongest in your life? The weakest? How does it compare with similar factors in your relationship with your earthly father? Have you separated the two relationships in your mind? In your heart?

8. Packer points out that, in adoption, establishing a child's legal status is only the beginning; making sure of a loving, trusting filial relationship is the real task for the parent. What new insights does this give us into what we can expect in our relationship with "Abba Father"? Discuss this statement: In our adoption into God's family we live out the greatness of God's grace.

9. The doctrine of adoption promises a share in Christ's glory. He is our elder brother, and we are "fellow heirs" (Rom. 8:17). Discuss the implications of being "like Him" when he appears (1 John 3:2)—physically, mentally, and spiritually.

10. The story in John 12:1-3 gives us a glimpse of a reunited Martha, Mary, and Lazarus. Because we have been adopted spiritually, we too can look forward to a family gathering in heaven as we meet with our "Abba Father" and our elder brother, Jesus. How are we instructed to regard the "trial of our faith" in the meantime? (See 1 Pet. 1:7.) What happens to gold when it goes through fire?

13

When Does the Joy Come?

JEHOVAH-SHAMMAH:
God is there

Imagine an imposing church structure fronted by an
elegant pillared porch. In your mind's eye, see two of those
stately white columns. Visualize their strength. Reach out
and feel their solidity.

This picture of permanence comes to mind when I think
of Tom and Mary Billman, two spiritual pillars of the
church my family and I have attended for more than
twenty years. They are such an integral part of the church
that I find it hard to imagine life at Immanuel Alliance
without them.

Are you thinking of an on-the-go couple who is present
at every function, involved in every church activity? Well,
Tom *is* Sunday school superintendent and church board
president, and that certainly involves a lot of work. Some
months, however, Mary may attend only one or two
services. Other months Mary is not able to attend at all.

When she is absent from church, we miss Mary's vibrant
sense of humor. We miss her ready laugh. For years we
have missed her gifted piano playing. We know that Tom
misses her presence by his side.

Since 1973 Mary has been a victim of Systemic Lupus
Erythematosus.

Lupus is defined as follows: "a chronic inflammatory disease that strikes an individual's immune system and affects connective tissue. . . . Systemic Lupus . . . involves the internal organs and systems of the body."[1]

As a result of lupus, Mary now lives with these added complications: cardiomyopathy, I.H.S.S. (Idiopathic Hypertropic Subaortic Stenosis), collagen vascular disease, renal vasculitis, and convulsive disorder (epilepsy).

Mary explains her life-style:

Lupus affects the connective tissues throughout the body and usually causes damage to one of the vital organs. In my case there are three involved: the heart, kidneys, and central nervous system. There is no cure, but with proper medical attention, medication, care, and rest, it can sometimes be stabilized. It is a disease where you have periods of remission and where you have flare-ups. You have good days and bad days. It requires strict discipline of your activity and, with me, my diet.

I was told in 1984 that with this illness and particularly with all the complications I have, the prognosis is very grave, medically speaking. But I know the Lord is with me and will be with me and give me the strength and courage to face each day. "We are pressed on every side by troubles, but not crushed and broken. We are perplexed because we don't know why things happen as they do, but we don't give up and quit" (2 Cor. 4:8, TLB).

Through this illness the Lord has helped me in many areas of my life in which I am weak. Among them are patience, discipline, and humility. I'm also learning to accept help from others and to be thankful and appreciative for all I do have. I may not have great health, but I have so much else. I have found a deeper faith and trust in the Lord. I still have much to learn, but I do know you can and must trust the Lord for everything in your life. He will never, never fail you.

We can rejoice, too, when we run into problems and trials, for we know that they are good for us—they help us learn to be patient. And patience develops strength of character in us and helps us trust God more each time we use it and finally our hope and faith are strong and steady. Then, when that happens, we are able to hold our heads high no matter what happens and know that all is well, for we know how dearly God loves us, and we feel this warm love everywhere within us because God has given us the Holy Spirit to fill our hearts with his love. (Rom. 5:3-5, TLB, emphasis mine)

Notice the first three words of verse 3: "We can rejoice."

How can you rejoice when your kidneys do not function properly, your heart is also malfunctioning, you have a disease for which there is no cure, and they can only *try* to keep your condition stabilized with medication?

Then, to top it off, you must maintain a rigid sodium-free diet which, in a few short words, eliminates everything that's good (like pizza, subs, ice cream, cake, etc.)!

I have asked myself many times over the past years: How can I rejoice?

My interpretation of rejoice is this: We can rejoice that we know the Lord and that He will sustain us and never forsake us in our suffering or trial. *He is always there.*

Always take a day at a time. The Lord will never give you more than you can handle; He will give you strength and courage for each day.

There is a lesson—and a blessing—in everything. Don't miss it! Learn from it.

Suffering can bring you closer to God, but beware! The enemy is always nearby to rob you of that closeness. We may not get the answer we want, but God's ways are always best. He knows what's ahead; we don't. In God there is always hope. Trust and be patient!

A challenge I often give myself is: *Imagine facing this illness—or any trial—without the Lord.* Psalm 34:19 tells us that "the good man does not escape all troubles—he has them too. But the Lord helps him in each and every one" (TLB).

Finally, the two most important steps to take when facing trials and suffering are these: Pray about everything, and thank God for every blessing and answer along the way.

Mary has allowed God to turn her *misery into ministry.* When she is able, on good days, to visit hospital patients and other members of the church who are experiencing difficulties, Mary and Tom know how to talk about suffering. They don't avoid unpleasant topics like physical and emotional pain. They can say with honesty: "We've been there. We're in this with you. You can count on our prayers."

It's *when we've been there* that we are best able to help others.

What a wonderful God we have—he is the Father of our Lord Jesus Christ, the source of every mercy, and the one who so wonderfully comforts and strengthens us in our hardships and trials. And why does he do this? So that when others are troubled, needing our sympathy and encouragement, we can pass on to them this same help and comfort God has given us. You can be sure that the more we undergo sufferings for Christ, the more he will shower us with his comfort and encouragement. . . . He will give you the strength to endure. (2 Cor. 1:3-7, TLB)

HOW CAN I REJOICE?

Mary's question is a haunting one, asked by countless people in differing crises: How can I rejoice?

Yes, God has promised comfort, encouragement, and strength to endure—but sometimes, when our arms and our pockets are empty, that promise seems a mockery. Hope of ever helping anyone else seems light-years away.

I've cried all night . . . When does the joy come?

Another Mary must have asked those questions. A Mary who, as a small-town teenager, faced some mind-boggling problems: How can I have a baby when I've never known a man intimately? Will I be able to convince Joseph that I have not been unfaithful to him? Who among the villagers will believe me? With the possibility of stoning (the Hebrew punishment for adultery) confronting me, how can I rejoice?

Mary was "greatly troubled and disturbed and confused" (Luke 1:29).

And yet God through His angel had said: "Hail, O favored one (endued with grace), the Lord is with you! Blessed—favored of God—are you before all other women!" (Luke 1:28).

Thirty-three years later, standing before a cross, Mary must have asked again: "How can I rejoice?"

Especially when her dying Son cried, "My God, My God, why have You forsaken Me?" (Mark 15:34).

His words keep ringing in my ears,
Recalling earlier times and fears.
He was about Your business then,
Explaining Your commands to men.
I would have torn Him from the cross
And saved the world from this great loss,
Had I the power.
But You left Him there!
You are His Father—don't You care?[2]

Those may have been Mary's thoughts. Whatever her feelings, Jesus was fully aware of them, even from the cross, but He did not protect her from pain. Nor from its purgative effects.

God did not spare His own Son—a part of the Elohim— the agony of suffering. It was in His plan of redemption to provide us *a Mediator who has been through all of earth's suffering, who is in it with us now.* "For we do not have a high priest who is unable to sympathize with our weaknesses, but we have one who has been tempted in every way, just as we are—yet was without sin" (Heb. 4:15, NIV). "God has said, 'I will never, *never* fail you nor forsake you'" (Heb. 13:5, TLB).

But when does the joy come? Dr. James Packer has a fitting answer:

Joy depends first on recognizing that Christ's death for us on Calvary is the all-time guarantee to us of our heavenly Father's love, and second, on accepting the limits imposed by our relative powerlessness and ignorance.

John, in C. S. Lewis's Pilgrim's Regress, *runs away from all that he was taught in his youth, but later he returns or regresses to humble Christian faith under the guidance of a wisdom he didn't have when he fled from it. Chastened, he stops rejecting and rebelling, and quiet joy breaks in.* [3]

In the first chapter I described my search for "that magical, mystical, spiritual experience that would somehow make the joy come"—the experience that always seemed to elude me or, at least, proved only temporary in its joy-producing benefits.

At that point in my life, would I have recognized the truth in the following statement?

Joy isn't strictly a feeling. It's a state of mind in which you're content with what you've got and you wouldn't exchange it for the world. This state of mind presupposes acceptance of the limits that God lays upon us. What limits? First, our inability to control events and our ignorance of God's plans; second, the inescapability of strain and pain; third, the certainty that nonetheless everything counts, so that one day, when God brings everything in judgment, we will all discover that what we choose to be and do in this world has determined our destiny for us. [4]

Mary of Nazareth recognized her inability to control events and her ignorance of God's plans. She accepted the inevitable strain and pain. Her earlier decision determined her immediate and eternal destiny: "Behold the handmaid of the Lord; be it unto me according to thy word" (Luke 1:38, KJV).

Because Mary implicitly trusted God's will for her life, in her body "the Word was made flesh . . ." (John 1:14, KJV). That child became a man who "dwelt among us" (John 1:14, KJV). The Hebrew word for dwell is the root word from which comes *Shekinah*, meaning the dwelling, abiding presence of the Lord on earth.

HIS ABIDING PRESENCE

So we come to the last name of God we will discuss. Jehovah-shammah: He is there! And, as we have seen, He was there all along.

He was there as Elohim in the Garden of Eden, creating Adam and Eve.

He was there as Jehovah, longing for fellowship with those He had created in righteousness and holiness, seeking them in love.

He was there as El Shaddai with childless Sarah and lonely Abraham, and later, with Naomi as well, in might and power—and tender nurturing, fulfilling His promise.

He was there as Jehovah-jireh with the outcast Hagar, providing water and encouragement for her and her son.

He was there as Jehovah-raah to lead the beautiful shepherdess Rachel and her passionate husband Jacob through the valley of the shadow of death.

He was there as Jehovah-rapha to use Miriam the cheerleader—now Miriam the leper—as an example of the results of a critical spirit.

He was there as Ishi and Adonai to teach two husbands—David and Hosea—the true meaning of repentance and love.

He was there as Jehovah-sabaoth when Hannah's private battle appeared totally uneven, and defeat seemed certain.

He was there as Jehovah-nissi to convince Moses and Joshua that His power was mightier than the past.

He was there as Jehovah-shalom to show through Gideon the need for obedience, even when it meant alienation and persecution.

He was there as El Elyon and El Roi when a burnt-out prophet wanted to break away—or break down.

He was there as Jehovah-M'Kaddesh and Jehovah-tsidkenu to cleanse and consecrate desolate victims of sin.

He was there as Abba Father when two heartbroken sisters lost their only brother.

He was there as a Baby in a frightened teenager's virgin body.

He was there . . . as Jehovah-shammah He *is* there . . . and He will be there!

This name is given in Ezekiel 48:35: "The name of the city [Jerusalem] from that day and ever after shall be, THE LORD IS THERE."

What makes this last name so pertinent to this chapter is that Ezekiel was speaking from Babylon, the land where the Hebrew people were being held in captivity.

Captivity can be physical, emotional, or spiritual. Corrie ten Boom, in her bitterness toward her German captors, found that God does not always immediately release us from these captivities. He simply promises to *be there with us*!

But the Hebrews kept forgetting His presence. They were a prime example of the old saying, "Familiarity breeds contempt."

They did not practice the knowledge of His presence. They ignored the laws laid down for their protection. They closed their ears to His prophets' warnings.

Finally, God's Spirit was too grieved to remain among them. The Hebrew word for "a jealous God" is *Qanna*. His jealousy is not human, but holy.

Ezekiel tells the story:

The Spirit lifted me up between earth and heaven and in visions of God he took me to Jerusalem . . . where the idol that provokes to jealousy stood. . . .

And he said to me, "Son of man, do you see what they are
doing—the utterly detestable things the house of Israel is doing
here, things that will drive me far from my sanctuary?"
. . . Then the glory of the Lord departed from . . . the temple.
(Ezek. 8:3, 6; 10:18, NIV)

The *Shekinah* glory of the Lord departed from Israel.
God's Spirit left grievingly, reluctantly. He could no longer
dwell among a people polluted with lust, adultery, child
sacrifice, and unashamed disobedience.

But He left a promise for the future with another Old
Testament prophet, Zechariah:

Shout and be glad, O Daughter of Zion. For I am coming, and I
will live among you. . . . Many nations will be joined with the
Lord in that day and will become my people. I will live among
you and you will know that the Lord Almighty has sent me to
you. (Zech. 2:10-11, NIV)

Six hundred years passed. The *Shekinah* glory came to
dwell on earth once again—this time in a tabernacle of
flesh, a human body that began in the womb of a
frightened teenager whose life "had found favor with God."

"When the fullness of the time was come, God sent forth
his Son, made of a woman . . . that we might receive the
adoption of sons" (Gal. 4:4-5, KJV).

But this was not the coming that Zechariah had
promised. Another "fullness of time" is ahead, a future
dwelling of the *Shekinah* glory among us. John tells of the
foretaste he was given of this time in Revelation 21:1-4
(NIV):

Then I saw a new heaven and a new earth. . . .
I saw the Holy City, the new Jerusalem, coming down out of
heaven from God, prepared as a bride beautifully dressed for her
husband.
And I heard a loud voice from the throne saying, "Now the
dwelling of God is with men, and he will live with them. They

will be his people, and God himself will be with them and be their God. He will wipe every tear from their eyes. There will be no more death or crying or pain, for the old order of things has passed away. (Emphasis mine)

We have seen how humans have disobeyed Jehovah . . . laughed in the face of El Shaddai . . . rebelled against Adonai . . . crucified a part of the Elohim.   But He still desires to dwell among us. He will come again and make all things new!

All creation is waiting patiently and hopefully for that future day when God will resurrect his children. For on that day thorns and thistles, sin, death, and decay . . . will all disappear, and the world around us will share in the glorious freedom from sin which God's children enjoy. . . .
And even we Christians, although we have the Holy Spirit within us as a foretaste of future glory, also groan to be released from pain and suffering. We, too, wait anxiously for that day when God will give us our full rights as his children, including the new bodies he has promised us—bodies that will never be sick again and will never die. (Rom. 8:19-21, 23, TLB)

The nights of weeping will be over. Forever over.
The morning will dawn on a new day, a day with no more death. No more crying. No more pain.
A day of joy! Look ahead and sing with me.
"Sing and rejoice, O daughter of Zion; for lo, I come, and I will dwell in the midst of you, says the Lord" (Zech. 2:10).
Jehovah-shammah! *He is there!*

WHAT IS THE MEANING OF HIS NAME?
1. What questions must have gone through Mary's mind when she learned of her unplanned pregnancy? What was her audible reply? (See Luke 1:38.)

2. "He that spared not his own Son, but delivered him up for us all, how shall he not with him also freely give us all things?" (Rom. 8:32, KJV). Does this promise necessarily entail material blessings here on earth?

3. According to Dr. James Packer, what limits does God set upon us?

4. What is the meaning of *Shekinah*?

5. One of God's names is *Qanna,* meaning "a jealous God." Describe human jealousy (as compared to holy jealousy). Finish this sentence: "Jealousy without holiness would be . . ."

6. The Greek word for dwell is *tabernacle.* Realizing that in Old Testament times God dwelt in a tent, how does this throw new light on the meaning of Romans 12:1-2? Read also 2 Corinthians 5:1-4.

7. When told by their Babylonian captors to sing while in captivity, the Hebrews wept, hung their harps on the willows by the rivers, and wailed: "How shall we sing the Lord's song in a strange land?" (Ps. 137:4). Have you experienced times when you stopped using your spiritual gifts—you hung your "harp" on the willows—because you could not sense God's presence? Where are you keeping your harp *now*?

8. Does God promise immediate deliverance from all captivity? What does He promise? (See Heb. 4:15.)

9. Because He is there in our captivities, Jehovah-shammah is able to turn *miseries into ministries.* Can you identify an example of this reversal in your own life? If not, is there a "misery" you need to give to your Abba to use as He sees fit? (See 2 Cor. 1:3-7.)

10. Is the description of the "city of God" in Psalm 46:4 meant to be literal? How does it correspond to Ezekiel's vision in Ezekiel 43:1-7 and John's vision in Revelation 21:1-3? What hope do these prophecies give us for the future?

NOTES

CHAPTER ONE
1. James I. Packer, *Knowing God* (Downers Grove, Ill.: InterVarsity Press, 1973), 6.
2. Joy Jacobs, *They Were Women, Too* (Camp Hill, Penn.: Christian Publications, 1981), 1.

CHAPTER TWO
1. Jacobs, *They Were Women, Too,* 4.
2. Lawrence J. Crabb, Jr., *Effective Biblical Counseling* (Grand Rapids: Zondervan, 1977), 61. Used by permission.
3. Jacobs, *They Were Women, Too,* 5.
4. Karen Burton Mains, *Karen! Karen!* (Wheaton, Ill.: Tyndale House, 1979), 13.
5. Nathan J. Stone, *Names of God* (Chicago: Moody Press, 1944), 34.
6. Deb Jackson, "The Fire," *Simply Love* (The Benson Company, 1981), sound recording.
7. Crabb, *Effective Biblical Counseling,* 70.
8. Stone, *Names of God,* 33.

CHAPTER THREE
1. W. Phillip Keller, *A Shepherd Looks at Psalm 23* (Grand Rapids: Zondervan, 1970), 26. Used by permission.
2. Keller, *A Shepherd Looks at Psalm 23,* 32-33.
3. Jacobs, *They Were Women, Too,* 10.
4. Crabb, *Effective Biblical Counseling,* 91-92.

CHAPTER FOUR
1. Crabb, *Effective Biblical Counseling,* 102.
2. Crabb, *Effective Biblical Counseling,* 106.
3. Jacobs, *They Were Women, Too,* 18.

CHAPTER FIVE
1. Jacobs, *They Were Women, Too,* 33.
2. Karen Burton Mains, "Infidelity," *Decision* magazine (March 1984).
3. Jacobs, *They Were Women, Too,* 52.
4. Ibid.
5. David A. Seamands, *Healing for Damaged Emotions* (Wheaton, Ill.: Victor Books, 1981), 85.
6. Jacobs, *They Were Women, Too,* 52.
7. Seamands, *Healing for Damaged Emotions,* 101.
8. Crabb, *Effective Biblical Counseling.*

CHAPTER SIX
1. Crabb, *Effective Biblical Counseling,* 71.
2. See 1 Chronicles 6:33-34. The Kohathites were the most honorable house of Levi.
3. Jacobs, *They Were Women, Too,* 28.
4. Crabb, *Effective Biblical Counseling,* 70.
5. Ibid.
6. The following books may be helpful in understanding and using your gifts:
Marion Duckworth, *Becoming Complete: Embracing Your Biblical Image* (Portland, Oreg.: Multnomah, 1985).
Kenneth Cain Kinghorn, *Discovering Your Spiritual Gifts* (Grand Rapids, Mich.: Zondervan, 1981).
Rick Yohn, *Discover Your Spiritual Gift and Use It* (Wheaton, Ill.: Tyndale House, 1981).
John E. Packo, *Find and Use Your Spiritual Gifts* (Camp Hill, Penn.: Christian Publications, 1980).
Kari Malcolm, *Women at the Crossroads* (Downers Grove, Ill.: InterVarsity Press, 1982).

CHAPTER SEVEN
1. David A. Seamands, *Healing of Memories* (Wheaton, Ill.: Victor Books, 1985), 12.
2. Ibid., 24.
3. Arnold R. Fleagle, "What Is in Thy Hand?" Sermon presented at Immanuel Christian & Missionary Alliance Church, Mechanicsburg, Penn., April 1986.
4. Henry H. Halley, *Halley's Bible Handbook* (Grand Rapids: Zondervan, 1965), 127.

CHAPTER EIGHT
1. Used by permission.
2. Seamands, *Healing for Damaged Emotions,* 82-83.
3. Jacobs, *They Were Women, Too,* 45.

CHAPTER NINE
1. Jacobs, *They Were Women, Too,* 26.
2. Ibid.
3. Elizabeth Moberly, *Homosexuality: A New Christian Ethic* (Greenwood, S.C.: Attic Press, 1983), 2.
4. Leanne Payne, *The Broken Image* (Westchester, Ill.: Crossway Books, 1981), 29. Used by permission of Good News Publishers/Crossway Books, Westchester, Illinois 60153.
5. Miriam Neff, *Women and Their Emotions* (Chicago: Moody Press, 1983), 63.

6. Rick Grant, "Lesbianism: How Understanding and Healing Can Bring Change," *Virtue* (September 1985), 44.
7. The following books may be helpful in understanding homosexuality: Leanne Payne, *The Broken Image* (Westchester, Ill.: Crossway Books, 1981). Elizabeth Moberly, *Homosexuality: A New Christian Ethic* (Greenwood, S.C.: Attic Press, 1983).
Colin Cook, *Homosexuality: An Open Door* (Boise, Idaho: Pacific Press, 1985).
8. Amy Carmichael, *Edges of His Ways* (London: S.P.C.K., 1955; Ft. Washington, Penn.: Christian Literature Crusade, 1975), 6. Used by permission.
9. Ibid.

CHAPTER TEN
1. "Incest: The Family Secret," *The Last Days Newsletter*, vol. 8, no. 1, 12-20. (Copyright 1985 by Last Days Ministries, Box 40, Lindale, TX 75771-0040. All rights reserved.)
2. For a more detailed study of these stories, read chapter 13 in my book *They Were Women, Too* (Camp Hill, Penn.: Christian Publications, 1981).
3. Eugenia Price, *The Unique World of Women* (Grand Rapids: Zondervan, 1969), 51. Used by permission of the author.
4. Susan Forward and Craig Buck, *Betrayal of Innocence* (New York: Penguin Books, 1978), 91. Originally published by Jeremy P. Tarcher Inc., Los Angeles. Used by permission.
5. "Incest: The Family Secret," *The Last Days Newsletter*.
6. Joy Jacobs, *They Were Women Like Me* (Englewood Cliffs, N.J.: Prentice-Hall, 1985), 23-24.
7. Stone, *Names of God*, 126.

CHAPTER ELEVEN
1. R. Kent Hughes, *Abba Father: The Lord's Pattern for Prayer* (Westchester, Ill.: Crossway Books, 1986), 27. Used by permission of Good News Publishers/Crossway Books, Westchester, Illinois 60153.

CHAPTER TWELVE
1. Elisabeth Elliot, *Passion and Purity* (Old Tappan, N.J.: Fleming H. Revell, 1984), 84. Used by permission of Fleming H. Revell Company.
2. Jacobs, *They Were Women Like Me*, 119-120.
3. Oswald Chambers, *My Utmost for His Highest* (N.Y.: Dodd, Mead & Co., 1949), 311.
4. Packer, *Knowing God*, 182-184.
5. Christine Wyrtzen, "My Father's House," *Person to Person* (Loveland Music, 1986), sound recording.
6. James Packer, *Your Father Loves You* (Wheaton, Ill.: Harold Shaw, 1986), May 6 reading. Copyright 1986 by James Packer and Jean Watson.

CHAPTER THIRTEEN
1. Lupus Foundation of America, Inc. *How Much Do You Know About Lupus?* (Washington, D.C.).
2. Jacobs, *They Were Women Like Me*, 205.
3. Packer, *Your Father Loves You*, July 9 reading.
4. Ibid.